A SIXTH SENSE

FOR PROJECT MANAGEMENT

AuthorHouse™
1663 Liberty Drive
Bloomington, IN 47403
www.authorhouse.com
Phone: 1-800-839-8640

First published by AuthorHouse   2/9/2011

ISBN: 978-1-4567-3044-4 (sc)
ISBN: 978-1-4567-3045-1 (dj)
ISBN: 978-1-4567-3043-7 (e)

Library of Congress Control Number: 2011900817

Printed in the United States of America

Any people depicted in stock imagery provided by Thinkstock are models, and such images are being used for illustrative purposes only. Certain stock imagery © Thinkstock.

This book is printed on acid-free paper.

Because of the dynamic nature of the Internet, any Web addresses or links contained in this book may have changed since publication and may no longer be valid. The views expressed in this work are solely those of the author and do not necessarily reflect the views of the publisher, and the publisher hereby disclaims any responsibility for them.

In Memory of Dad,
George H. Roeder Jr.

To Elizabeth, Garrett, and Parker

CONTENTS

FOREWORD

This is an important book for a number of reasons.

Firstly, although project management is still a maturing discipline within the management domain, it is increasingly seen as one way in which progressive organizations can differentiate themselves. Even so, our knowledge of the way that project-based management engages with more traditional management styles is still evolving, meaning that although we are arguably getting better at understanding project-based work, we have a long way to go.

There are of course tools to manage the maturity of project processes (the Project Management Institute (PMI)'s OPM3®, for example). Still, it is evident that as project maturity improves, it requires a shift from the "tools and techniques" of the project world toward an environment where interpersonal skills and behaviors are more highly developed and applied. It could be argued that this shift away from the traditional project paradigm based on the PMI *Body of Knowledge* (PMBOK®) toward a more nuanced and behaviorally driven means of leading and managing project-based work is more akin to the work of mechanics— who follow process and repetition—being replaced by artists, who use flair, creativity, and expertise to move beyond traditional models of achieving. That shift is captured here.

Secondly, Tres Roeder has identified his six key elements, or disciplines,that contribute to successful project and change implementation based on significant experience, practical testing, and a reliance on the underlying academic theory. This ensures that the opinions expressed here are robustly supported out there in the real world.

Those disciplines (Awareness, Whole Body Decisions™, Clear Communication, Adaptability, Diplomacy, and Persistence) are all interpersonally and behaviorally based and offer a pathway to an evolving set of skills that are demonstrably helpful to project success. Although we are all still wrestling with the challenges of surviving and thriving in the current difficult organizational environment, there is much here that can assist and maybe even resolve the issues of complexity and ambiguity in the modern progressive organization.

I am also personally gratified that *A Sixth Sense for Project Management* addresses the power of intuition within the project domain. Often we see intuition in terms of experience.The experienced project manager or leader will certainly benefit froma personal library of previously successful interventions that can be creatively adapted to resolve project issues, together with an intuitive gut feel for which of these will be the most effective in a given situation. I also have to own up here—this is one of mypersonal research interests.

Thirdly, and perhaps most importantly, *A Sixth Sense for Project Management* is very persuasive in its premise that of all the core project management characteristics or competencies valued by project managers, it is the behavioral ones that are the most valued. Most of us working or researching in the project domain have our own views of what contributes to project success, and there has been a real shift over the past decade away from a dependence on the tools and techniques of project-based management, and toward the softer skills that project managers develop over time and with experience.

Even so, this shift is an uncomfortable one for the Project Management Institute, and for the PMBOK®, as it brings into question the focus on process that the PMBOK® encapsulates and promotes. Also, there has been a broadly accepted assumption, especially among practicing project managers, that the Project Management Professional (PMP®) qualification, which is largely based on knowledge of the PMBOK®, assists those project managers in the execution of their work. However, literally in the last few days, empirical evidence has emerged that refutes this.

In February of 2011, the *Project Management Journal*—the PMI's own research journal—published an empirical research study by Jo Ann Starkweather and Deborah Stevenson of Northeastern State University, which statistically demonstrated that of fifteen core PM competencies, PMP® certification is the least valued. This is an important validation of the theme and content of *A Sixth Sense for Project Management*, and is bound to be the source of much debate.

So, having received some important validation of the scope and content of this text, I hope you enjoy it and learn from it.

I know that I did!

Dr. Steve Leybourne, PhD
BOSTON UNIVERSITY
2 February 2011

Starkweather, J.A.& Stevenson, D.H. (2011) PMP® "Certification as a Core Competency: Necessary But Not Sufficient,"*Project Management Journal* 42,no. 1 (February): 31-41.

"We must learn to work with people as they are …
since we can't have them as we wish."

George Washington

A CALL FOR CHANGE

A PROFESSION IN TROUBLE

A Sixth Sense for Project Management® is Roeder Consulting's framework for managing the human side of change. Deploying A Sixth Sense for Project Management®, Roeder Consulting has led client projects to successful outcomes 90 percent of the time. Considering all of the variables in people and projects, we feel good about these results.

Throughout this book, I will reference Roeder Consulting and our work because it will be helpful for you to understand what our company does. In short, we are a ten-person consulting and training firm focused on helping clients change successfully. We measure ourselves by the metric in the first paragraph of this book. Did we lead the client's project to a successful outcome? Did we help the people in our training programs lead their organization's to a successful outcome? After some ten years of working on major change initiatives for a variety of organizations, I have grown to appreciate the absolute criticality of properly managing the human side of change.

I worked on projects for many Fortune 500 clients. I do not discuss the names of the clients in this book for confidentiality reasons. Some Fortune 500 projects I personally worked on have been front-page news in the *Wall Street Journal*. Others have been highlighted by the chief executive officer in the annual report for positively contributing to the company's performance. I mention these details only to provide perspective on the size and scope of projects I have been involved with. I also led projects for midsize and small corporations and not-for-profit organizations.

In all cases, projects and change are about people. People skills are so important that I began a personal journey to learn how to manage people during times of change. I call the contents of that body of knowledge A Sixth Sense for Project Management®. Later, I will share more details on the story of how I created A Sixth Sense for Project Management®.

Today, Roeder Consulting trains thousands of project managers and other leaders of change on these principles. A number of these people personally tell me that our approach has altered the way they think about managing change. One of the most satisfying times this occurred was earlier this year in Charlotte, North Carolina. I had just completed a training course to a group of almost twenty-five people. One of the gentlemen in the room had spent his career managing projects. He had, perhaps, twenty-five or thirty years of experience and he was on his second training course from Roeder Consulting. He told me our programs had caused him to rethink his approach.

The Sixth Sense tools and techniques we are using can be applied by all project managers. We are not doing anything you can't do. This book will outline the steps you can take to improve your rate of successful implementations too.

Research shows that many projects fail. One commonly quoted research study from the Standish Group reports that, on average, only 32 percent of all information technology projects succeed. Clearly, project management is a profession that must do better. In section one, I will discuss how we ended up in this environment of high project failures. Also, I will share a brief history of A Sixth Sense for Project Management® and how it fits into a balanced approach. Finally, in this section I will ask you to join me in embracing the changes we must make to elevate the profession of project management to the next level.

What Is a "Project Manager?"

This book frequently uses the term "project manager." By this term, I am referring not only to people who are professionally certified as project managers by the Project Management Institute (PMI) or a similar other group, but also to the much larger audience of people who find themselves leading projects. This larger group includes, but is not limited to, organizational consultants, business analysts, many human resources professionals, executives, and people of all kinds of backgrounds in roles at not-for-profit organizations. When you stop to think about it, much of what we do in life is a project. And much of what you do may be referred to as "project management."

PMI created a standard for managing projects called the Project Management Body of Knowledge (PMBOK® Guide). According to the PMBOK® Guide, "a project is a temporary endeavor undertaken to create a unique product, service, or result." If you are conducting work that meets this criterion, then you are a project manager. "Project manager" may not formally be in your title, and you may not even be employed, but that's what you are doing. Perhaps you volunteer with a parent-teacher organization and are in charge of the annual picnic. That's a project. Perhaps you are on the swim team and need to arrange transportation for the local swim meet. That's a project. Each of these activities has a defined beginning, a defined end, and a definite result that must be achieved.

Finally, I use the term "project manager" and "project leader" interchangeably. I believe people who manage projects *are* leaders.

Many Projects Fail—Lack of People Skills Is a Primary Reason

Only 32 percent of information technology projects, as I already stated, are successful. This troubling statistic is the result of the extensive research of the Standish Group. Standish compiled these results from over 70,000 IT projects. Even more troubling, our performance is not improving. The success rate for projects six years earlier was 34 percent.

My experience has shown me that inadequate management of

people-related issues is often at the heart of project failure. One such area is lack of business ownership and accountability. Have you ever had a project where the executive sponsor did not support the project? I know from discussions in our public classes and webinars that projects typically do not succeed without business ownership and accountability. If we are going to reduce this cause of project failure, we need something more than what we are currently doing. We need A Sixth Sense for Project Management®.

Another cause of project failure is that the team lacks authority or decision-making ability. In Roeder Consulting's training programs, we have asked the following question for years: "Do all of the stakeholders in your projects report directly to you?" I have never met a project manager who answered that *every* stakeholder reports directly to him or her. We ask another question as a follow-up: "Do *any* of the stakeholders in your projects report directly to you?" Data from several of our global webinars, representing 776 respondents, showed that 76 percent of the audience did not have *any* of their project stakeholders reporting directly to them.

Project management is a profession of people who must accomplish results through *other people*. We need *other people* to approve our budget. We need *other people* to sign off on the scope of the project. It's not that we aren't capable of doing it. It's simply that this is the way the project management role is typically structured. Other people need to make decisions. Learning how to have other people support us is not a skill that we traditionally learn in project management training. If we are going to reduce project failure, we need something more than what we are currently doing. We need A Sixth Sense for Project Management®. In the remainder of this chapter, I will discuss the critical importance of the people skills that are embedded in A Sixth Sense for Project Management®.

The first piece of research that emphasizes the importance of A Sixth Sense for Project Management® comes from the doctoral studies of Dale Christenson, PhD. Dr. Christenson is one of the first people in the world to receive a PhD in project management. A tall gentleman with a large swath of hair parted on one side, his presence is formidable, as one might expect from the former assistant deputy minister and member of the Royal Canadian Mounted Police.

For his doctoral research, Dr. Christenson studied sixty-five peer-reviewed articles on successful projects. He scoured these articles for the common elements of project success. He found that seven "critical success factors" are consistently present when projects succeed. I have summarized each critical success factor below in roughly the order of importance. For example, senior management support is the most important critical success factor. Each critical success factor has a major people skills component.

Senior Management Support

Intellectual, financial, and political support from senior management provides a critical backdrop for project success. Senior managers who are also in project management roles are likely to use interpersonal skills to deliver results. As one's career advances, the importance of technical project management skills typically decreases as the importance of people skills increases. Project managers who are not senior managers, but must work with them, will also find that their interpersonal skills are important to successful relationships.

Clear Goals

Project teams are more likely to succeed when they know where they are going. Clear goals are primarily about business acumen and sixth sense people skills. Business acumen involves an understanding of how the project is tied to organizational goals and the specific elements of those goals the project will achieve. I will discuss business acumen in more detail in chapter three. Sixth sense people skills train you to learn a person's true goals in a project and gain alignment from all the key stakeholders on those goals.

Competent Project Manager

Regardless of an organization's tools, processes, culture, etc., the project manager must be skilled to deliver results. I have heard some organizations claim that they just need to set up the right system to manage projects. With the right software and processes, they argue, project management will succeed.

Dr. Christenson's research and my personal experience do not support this argument. Instead, they confirm that the project manager *does* make a difference. Regardless of how great an organization's systems and processes may be, there is still a need for a talented, well-trained project manager to deliver results.

Adequate Resources

Having adequate resources means having *enough* resources and having the *right* resources. The term *resources* applies to both human resources and financial resources. Identifying and securing the right resources is a sixth sense people skill. It calls on disciplines, such as these:

- Awareness—to determine what resources are needed.
- Clear Communication—to state your case for these resources.
- Diplomacy—to secure the resources.

Project Management Framework

The essence of this critical success factor is that we need a road map to guide us from project start to project completion. However, there is not one best project management framework. It is situational. I will address this in chapter seven when I discuss the Adaptability Discipline. The point I want to make here is that you are much more likely to succeed if you have *a framework*. Frameworks can be very simple or quite complex. Following a project framework is a technical skill. In chapter three, I will discuss technical skills in more detail. Knowing which framework to use and how to adapt it to your needs is a sixth sense people skill.

Control System

Your project management framework must be controlled. In other words, you need some sort of mechanism to ensure people are following the methodology. Further, you need a way to get people back on track when they stray from the methodology. A control system, like a project management framework, is a technical tool. Using the control system is a technical skill. Selecting the right control mechanism, adapting it to your needs, and knowing how to have the conversation with people when they stray from the methodology are all sixth sense people skills.

Project Vision

In addition to the above six critical success factors found in the current literature, Dr. Christenson argues that project vision is also a critical success factor. His research dissertation supports this proposition.

While I mentioned clear goals above as a critical success factor, it is vision that guides those goals. Vision tells us *why* we are doing what we are doing. A pedantic conversation about the definition of goals versus the definition of a vision is beyond the scope of this book. I have seen many clients spiral into hours of lost productivity arguing about the definition of terms such as these. The important point to grasp from this list of critical success factors is that someone, or some group of people, needs to clearly define why a project exists and what it is trying to accomplish. Let's call that a vision. The vision is particularly helpful when the specific path your team is on comes to a dead end. If you are guided by a vision, you can say, "Well, that road did not lead me to the vision. What other ways can I get there?"

This vision must be shared in order to be effective. Creating a shared vision is a major challenge for many organizations. Regrettably, different people and different divisions often operate in their own direction. Sometimes, in the worst cases, they are counteracting each other's efforts and working against what is good for the enterprise. A vision is clearly in the realm of business acumen—understanding the competitive marketplace and developing strategies to succeed as an organization. Articulating the vision is a communication skill and that puts it into the realm of sixth sense people skills. Furthermore, knowing how to adapt your approach when you reach a dead end is a sixth sense people skill.

In summary, all seven of Dr. Christenson's "critical success factors" have a people skills component.

More Evidence People Skills Are Present When Projects Succeed

Researching the Value of Project Management, coauthored by Mark Mullaly and Janice Thompson, showed that people skills correlate to project success. This study also showed that in some cases, when we do not adapt our approach (Adaptability is one of the six disciplines of A Sixth Sense for Project Management®), we may actually destroy project value. I discuss this research in more detail in chapter seven.

Listed below are several additional studies proving the positive correlation between the project manager's people skills and project success:

- "The primary problems of project managers are not technical but human. Improving project managers' technological capabilities will be helpful only to the extent that this improves their abilities to communicate, be organized, build teams, provide leadership, and deal comfortably with change." (Posner, 1987)

- "Personal competence may be a better predictor of a person's potential to perform … than functional competence." (Cheetham and Chivers, 1998)

- "The human side of project management is more important than the formal aspects." (Lechler, 1998)

- "Without mastering the timeless soft skills to supplement the hard skills … few project managers will succeed." (Jiang, 2002)

Further, it has been shown that the people skills required of project managers vary by project phase. According to project management professor Gregory Skulmoski from the College of Information Technology at Zayed University in Abu Dhabi, and project and program management professor Francis Hartman from the Zulich School of Engineering in Calgary, "Effective questioning and listening skills are critical at the start of a project in order to understand the business problem and preliminary requirements … (T)heir importance declines in the close-out phase in favor of writing skills."

In summary, there is an overwhelming body of evidence showing that people skills are critical to project success. Indeed, many studies show that people skills are more important than technical skills. Further, project managers must develop a portfolio of people skills to accommodate the varying needs of each phase of the project. One or two people skills will not do; we must possess a deep set of interpersonal capabilities. Clearly, successful project managers need A Sixth Sense for Project Management®.

BIRTH OF A SIXTH SENSE FOR PROJECT MANAGEMENT®

A Sixth Sense for Project Management® is a concept I started to develop about ten years ago. At the time, I was a consultant for Booz Allen Hamilton. I worked on a number of strategic engagements for well-known Fortune 500 companies. We developed detailed documents filled with strategic recommendations. In some cases, our clients would ask us to implement the strategies contained in these documents.

When those clients asked us to implement strategies, I thought I knew how to do it. Prior to Booz Allen Hamilton, I worked in industry for about ten years in sales, marketing, and operations roles. I implemented changes in the areas I was responsible for. Also, I earned a master's in business administration from the Kellogg Graduate School of Management in Chicago. My training there included courses in organizational behavior and change.

I remember thinking, *How difficult can implementation be?* Implementation, I thought, was a matter of sharing the strategic document with people, pointing them in the right direction, and dealing with the occasional hiccup. How wrong I was. I learned from the school of hard knocks that implementation is incredibly difficult. I decided to become more sophisticated in how I approached implementation. Indeed, I devoted my professional life to becoming an expert implementer of strategy.

I left Booz Allen Hamilton and started my own business, Roeder Consulting. My goal for Roeder Consulting from day one was to focus on implementation. I saw first-hand that the skills required to formulate strategy are very different from those required to implement strategy. Many formulators of strategy saw the implementation piece as an afterthought. I wanted to change that way of thinking. I wanted to create a firm that focused solely on how to take strategic ideas, refine them, and make them happen. Our main metric would be whether or not the strategy was implemented. I began tracking our projects and success rates. The 90 percent success rate I mentioned in chapter one is the result of these efforts.

I found implementation work invigorating and fascinating. You may have heard the saying, "I wish these meetings would end so I can get real work done." Talking with people and working them through the new order of things, in my profession, *is* the real work. Sure, there are plenty of times when we need to be in front of computers to analyze data and prepare presentations. However, for successful implementation nothing beats interacting with people and working it out.

As I strived to professionalize my approach to implementation, I thought, *There must be someone or some group of people who have thought through a more organized way to manage these projects.* I went online and found a group called the Project Management Institute (PMI). PMI issues a professional certification called the Project Management Professional (PMP). I filled out all the paperwork, took the exam (not a fun way to spend a day), and earned my credential as a Project Management Professional.

At last, I thought, *now I really know how to lead change.* After all, I had a piece of paper that said so!

Shortly after successfully completing the certification test, I returned to the project I was working on. The project was large, complicated, and cross-functional. My first step as a newly minted PMP was to go to the Information Technology Department. Information Technology had a big role in developing software for this project. Most of the people in the IT group, unlike the rest of the organization, knew what a PMP credential was. *These are my people,* I thought. *They will get it.* I informed them we needed to figure out how much time their portion of the project was going to take. I asked them to help me break down the project into deliverables and work packages for the upcoming year. Then I went over to the Sales and Marketing Department. I am a former sales and marketing person. I thought I could communicate well to this group too. I said to the sales and marketing people, "Here's all that we need from you. Please tell me your availability so we can see how to fit you into our work plan." My plan was to take information from these groups and optimize the project. I was going to track *earned value,* a popular project management metric. I was going to figure out the critical path. I was going to do all the things I learned from the PMP training.

Go ahead and venture a guess as to how that project worked out. You guessed it. The answer is, "Not well." I learned that my technical PMP skills were important, but not sufficient to lead change. Also, I learned that any allegiance earned or relationships built in the past may as well fly out the window when it comes to change. I thought the IT group would appreciate my PMP credential. They cared deeply about the content of the new changes, but not so much about my credential. I thought the sales and marketing people would respect me as someone who had been in their shoes. It turned out that was not nearly as important as what I represented today, right now.

As I look back over the last ten years of leading major change projects, I can think of a number of cases where organizations put someone into a change leader position in charge of a group that he or she had an affinity with. In so many of these cases, the person thought this would earn him or her the trust and respect of peers. It did not. Sometimes, these people grew quite frustrated and saddened. They would ask me, "Why is everyone giving me such a hard time? I am one of them. They just need to trust me." The answer to that question is that all bets are off when it comes to change. People scatter in all directions. Your past experiences may help in some way, but *what* you do today and *how* you do it are the new measures people will use to evaluate you.

Now, let's go back to the story of my own learning curve. After earning an MBA and a PMP, I thought I understood strategy and how to lead projects. Yet my projects in many cases were still underperforming. I was at another crossroads in my career. I had a blind spot. My blind spot had to do with the human side of these projects. It had to do with politics, emotions, and differences in opinion. *Well*, I thought, *maybe it's just me.*

I hired a consultant to help me figure out what this blind spot was. He asked other project managers what they thought. Did they have this blind spot in their projects? Did they experience challenges with people? Had they seen emotional behavior? Did people challenge them on their projects? Overwhelmingly, the project managers we talked to and surveyed said, "Yes! We are experiencing these challenges in our projects too."

My interest perked up. I wanted to know more. We asked these project managers to give us more detail. We distributed a survey with a list of skills project managers might possess. We asked participants to grade how important each skill is, in their opinion. What follows is a list of the skills ranked according to what this group said was a "must have" skill for a project manager.

Skills	% Say "Must Have"
Questioning and listening skills, ascertaining and developing needs and key issues.	77%
Determining direction-taking initiative and running meetings.	76%
Using integrity and ethics in judgment about work and organizational issues.	76%
Being a self-starter, self-motivated, keeping focused and productive.	76%
Time management and being effective and productive.	74%
Managing relationships with customers and colleagues.	72%
Business writing: letters, quotations, proposals, confirmations, contracts, reports, etc.	71%
Delegation skills: assesses the capabilities of others and assigns work accordingly.	68%
Resilience: perseveres in the face of obstacles and adapts to change.	68%
Pro-activity: action orientation that leads to measurable results.	68%
Developing solutions with stakeholders, customers, vendors, and staff. Understanding and using unique selling points.	64%
Negotiating strategy techniques and skills so as to produce mutually positive outcomes.	63%
Handling stress, conflict, and pressure in a positive way.	63%
Developing positive relationships, cooperation with and supporting my colleagues.	61%
Risk taking: willing and capable of operating with uncertainty.	59%
Managing upward and sideways (my managerial superiors and my peers).	57%
Taking personal responsibility to resolve problems, even those not of my own making.	57%
Politics/influence: using various types of influence to build alliances, networks, allies.	53%
Creating and giving senior-level presentations to groups.	50%
Virtual teaming: managing persons and/or vendors at remote locations.	49%
Understanding the way people really feel beyond what they seem to be saying.	48%
Financial understanding: profit and loss, cash flow, variable/fixed costs, capital/revenue, depreciation, etc.	40%
Striving for new skills, knowledge, experience, and personal development.	37%

Exhibit 2-1 Project Manager "Must Haves"

The highest scored item in this list is "Questioning and listening skills, ascertaining and developing needs and key issues." Projects are put in place to deliver agreed-upon goals. It is encouraging to see a high percentage of the project managers who were surveyed recognizing the critical importance of doing a good job developing the project needs.

Several items down the list is "Being a self-starter, self-motivated, keeping focused and productive." Interestingly, 76 percent of project mangers felt this was a must-have. Later in this book, I will discuss Persistence as one of the six disciplines of A Sixth Sense for Project Management®. Certainly, the ability to keep oneself going is critical to the Persistence Discipline and project success.

Now, look at the item that project managers scored the lowest: "Striving for new skills, knowledge, experience, and personal development." I find it interesting that only 37 percent of the project managers we surveyed felt this was a "must have." Perhaps some people believe the discipline of project management is static. I view it differently. In order to get to the next level, we need to dramatically upgrade our professional "tool kit" to include not only the technical skills, but also business acumen and sixth sense people skills.

The second to last item listed is also interesting. Only 40 percent of project managers believe financial understanding to be a "must have." Financial acumen is part of business acumen. In my opinion, this is a critical skill for project managers to understand.

My "Ah-Ha" Moment

One day we were sitting in our office in Cleveland, Ohio, looking at the above research and other feedback we received. We had identified the blind spot. We were trying to name it. We knew that it was more than people skills. It certainly wasn't technical skills. Then, I had what you might call an "Ah-ha!" moment. I jumped up and said, "It's almost as if we need A Sixth Sense for Project Management®!" Well, that term stuck.

Also, this moment marks the beginning of my realization that there are three key skills one must possess to successfully lead change: technical skills, business acumen, and sixth sense people skills. Used together holistically, these three skills are the foundation of a successful project manager. In the next chapter, I will discuss each of these three skills in more detail. Together, I call them "The Balanced Approach."

Chapter 3

A CALL TO ACTION FOR A MORE BALANCED APPROACH

Chapter one demonstrated that project managers must have people skills to be successful in their projects. In chapter two, I shared my personal story where I learned that my education and credentialing were important but not sufficient. I needed to develop a third skill set focused on working with people during times of change. In this chapter, I will detail a balanced approach that combines the three core skills that project managers need to be successful:

- Technical skills (such as PMP certification);
- Business acumen (such as MBA training); and
- People skills (A Sixth Sense for Project Management® training).

I realize you may not be in a position to earn an MBA or professional certification as a project manager. That is okay because that depth of knowledge is not always required. However, if you are to succeed, you will want to have at least a minimum level of understanding in each of the three areas of business acumen, technical skills, and sixth sense people skills. You do not need to excel at all three, but you do need to be, at minimum, proficient at all three. For example, if you have great technical skills (such as PMP certification) but poor business acumen and poor people skills, then you are not likely to lead projects to successful outcomes.

Technical Skills

Technical skills are primarily what you learn if you are professionally certified as a project manager. Measuring earned value, templates for a charter, and creating and updating a project schedule are all examples of technical skills. These skills can also be developed without certification. For example, they can be learned through your employer. The organization you work with may have its own set of standards, templates, and tools. Additionally, technical skills can be learned through self-study or through working with experienced project managers. Technical skills are very important. But they are only one of three legs to the stool required for a balanced approach.

Business Acumen

Business acumen is the willingness and ability to take responsibility for your project's results and to know, at all times, how your project is helping the organization achieve at least one of its goals. At the 2008 PMI Global Congress in Denver, there was a presentation about the new Program Management Professional (PgMP) credential. The PgMP credential had just been released. A gentleman presenting to a room of several hundred people posed the following question to the group: "What if your project delivers on time, on budget, and within scope, but does absolutely nothing to deliver value to your organization? Whose problem is that?" Many in the audience began to shift uncomfortably in their chairs and I heard grumbling around the room. The people really did not think it was their problem. Finally, one brave soul stood up and slowly walked to the microphone. "That would be an executive problem," he said. Most people in the room laughed, showed support, and said "Yes! An executive problem! That's right!" I firmly disagree. I submit to you that it is *your* problem, regardless of whether it also is an executive problem. As project managers, in order to get our profession to the next level, we need to understand and be willing to accept responsibility for business results. That is what business acumen is all about.

Business acumen also includes an understanding of your organization's products and services. You do not need to be expert, but you should have a basic knowledge of what your organization does and the key drivers of how your organization delivers value. This basic understanding will help guide you in your projects. Project management should not operate as a separate silo that only gets involved with the technical aspects of projects, as is so often characteristic. We need to be aware of and knowledgeable about the business. This becomes critical in helping us determine how to deliver underlying value.

Projects are not a straight line. We know there will be curves in the road. If you understand your organization's products and services and what your organization's value proposition is, then this becomes your guiding light in difficult times. If you are not sure where to go with your projects, remind yourself what your organization does, and then let that inform your next steps. Always look for ways to deliver value.

Sixth Sense People Skills

People skills provide the third leg of the stool. Technical skills and business acumen are important. However, on their own, they are not sufficient. Successful project managers must master the human side of change.

Projects are about results. Successful project managers deliver results by combining these three core skills: technical skills, business acumen, and sixth sense people skills. Exhibit 3-1 visually shows how these pieces fit together:

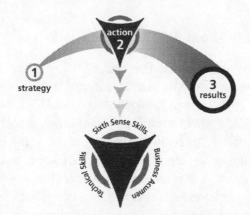

Exhibit 3-1 A Balanced Approach

What Does The PMBOK® Guide Say?

Let's take a look at the Project Management Body of Knowledge to see what it states about the human side of change. I'll start at the beginning. The PMBOK® Guide explains that managing a project includes the following:

- Identifying requirements;
- Addressing the various *needs, concerns, and expectations of the stakeholders* as the project is planned and carried out;
- *Balancing the competing project constraints* including, but not limited to; scope, quality, schedule, budget, resources, and risk.

I might add to this list that project management includes stress resulting in sleepless nights! All kidding aside, look at the second bullet point above. The authors of the PMBOK® Guide say that managing a project includes: "addressing the various needs, concerns and expectations of the stakeholders." I agree. However, does the PMBOK® Guide train us how to do that? No.

The PMBOK® Guide is focused on technical skills. We need to look elsewhere for training in effective people skills. However, the PMBOK® Guide does now recognize the importance of people skills. Let's look at the new addition to the latest version of the PMBOK® Guide, Appendix G.

One Final Note about the PMBOK® Guide

Appendix G is located near the end of the PMBOK® Guide. It says that, "Effective project managers acquire a balance of technical, interpersonal, and conceptual skills." It is a positive development that the PMBOK® Guide now formally acknowledges that there is more to leading change than the technical skills covered in the PMBOK® Guide. Roeder Consulting has been training people on a more balanced approach for years. It is reassuring to know that the PMBOK® Guide finally formally recognizes the importance of these skills. Consider the similarities between Appendix G and our balanced approach:

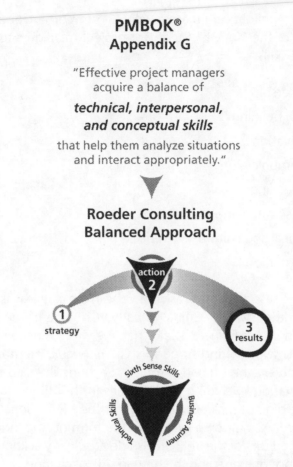

PMBOK®
Appendix G

"Effective project managers
acquire a balance of

technical, interpersonal,
and conceptual skills

that help them analyze situations
and interact appropriately."

Roeder Consulting
Balanced Approach

action
2

1
strategy

3
results

Sixth Sense Skills

Technical Skills

Business Acumen

Exhibit 3-2 Comparing Appendix G to
Roeder Consulting's Balanced Approach

Whereas Appendix G lists three areas of "technical, interpersonal, and conceptual skills," Roeder Consulting argues the three core skills are "technical, business acumen, and sixth sense people skills." We combine interpersonal skills, conceptual skills, adaptability, and a host of other interpersonal attributes into sixth sense people skills. Further, we add business acumen to the list because we believe this is critical. As mentioned previously, we must accept responsibility as a profession for project results. We must understand the underlying value proposition of our organizations. These skills are called business acumen.

Appendix G highlights eight areas where it's important, according to the authors of the PMBOK® Guide, for project managers to develop their people skills:

- Leadership
- Team building
- Motivation
- Communication
- Influencing
- Decision-making
- Political and cultural awareness
- Negotiation

In our training sessions, I often ask if anyone in the course was involved with writing the PMBOK® Guide. In early 2010, one of the students in a program in San Francisco said that she was. Coincidentally, she was involved with writing Appendix G. She was a member of the team working on the human resources section. She said the team felt strongly about including people skills in the HR section. Those people skills did not make the final cut for the HR section. However, they did become their own section in the form of Appendix G. The authors and editors of the PMBOK® Guide are clearly acknowledging the importance of managing the human side of change.

Calling on Our Profession to Do Better

Available literature and studies demonstrate in great depth the virtues of people skills. Upon reflection on this, it is interesting to ask why, as a profession, we focus so much on just one aspect of professional project management: the project management framework and technical skills.

If you could learn only one skill to lead change, the most impactful set of skills to learn would be the sixth sense people skills. Empirical evidence, as I mentioned in chapter one, shows people skills correlate to project success, *not* the technical skills. This may be contrary to conventional wisdom in the project management profession. Today, there is much focus on professional certifications that are based on technical skills. More companies are requiring technical skill certification for their project managers. Yet this focus is on the one leg of the stool that, arguably, is the smallest and weakest. I believe this evidence points out a need for us to rethink our priorities as a profession. There should be much more emphasis on the people side of change.

Changes to Certification?

I believe this begs several important questions. Should people skills be a larger part of the certification process? Should some of the Professional Development Units (PDUs) required for recertification be required to be people skills related? Mastering people skills is a lifelong journey. Ongoing work on our people skills is important. I call on us as a profession to have a meaningful dialogue on this topic. In a recent webinar, I asked a group of 380 project managers from around the world to answer the following question: "Should people skills be a required component of project management training?" *An overwhelming 98 percent* of the attendees answered yes. Clearly, something needs to be done to increase our attention to people skills in managing the human side of change.

Also, should executives, project management office leaders, and others who control training budgets ensure that their staffs become trained on people skills? I think so. I would argue for people skills *first* and project management framework second. As a registered education provider for the Project Management Institute, I am on a distribution list for requests for proposals from all sorts of companies and organizations. An informal scan indicates that most organizations new to project management ask for training on technical skills. Why?

Perhaps it's the result of four decades of emphasis on technical skills. We now understand project management better than we ever have. We know that people skills are more highly correlated to successful change than technical skills. Also, we know that those technical skills sometimes are the *cause* of failed projects. Technical skills training should come with a warning label: "Caution, these technical skills may lead to reduced project performance." Our technical skills can get us into trouble when we force our projects into some arbitrary project management framework, regardless of the project environment and the organizational culture.

A New Era in Project Management

We are entering a new era in project management. The last forty years have been characterized primarily by technical skills. Roeder Consulting reviewed forty years of project management doctrine. As we reviewed this doctrine, we categorized it into three buckets: technical skills, business acumen, and people skills. Forty years of project management doctrine primarily resides in technical skills. This doctrine has done a great job getting us to where we are today. But we know that many projects fail and the failure rate is increasing. We know that one of the reasons why many projects fail is because of a lack of people skills. We also know that when we succeed, we succeed because we are good at managing the human side of change.

The new era we are entering is characterized by a more balanced approach of technical skills, business acumen, and people skills. This is the path to reducing failure rates and increasing the status of the project management profession.

The coming years will determine whether we accept our responsibility for business results, as a profession, and grow into an expanded role that embraces business acumen and people skills. If you want to be part of the new era, please join us via social media or the newsletter service available through our website RoederConsulting.com. Let's work together to take our profession to the next level.

THE SIX DISCIPLINES

"Wisdom is not obvious."

Sun Tzu

Over a period of many years, Roeder Consulting's team of consultants and trainers endeavored to become expert on how to manage the human side of change. We pulled together scientific findings, real-world experiences, and project management fundamentals. The result is six disciplines that define A Sixth Sense for Project Management®. Listed below are just several examples of the due diligence behind these disciplines:

- Participated in the first NeuroLeadership Conference held in the beautiful setting of Asolo, Italy. This invitation-only summit pulled together top neurologists, psychologists, CEOs, and business practitioners to discuss the science of change.

- Analyzed numerous scholarly articles about the human side of change. Roeder Consulting incorporates science into its approach because we want to have reasonable assurance that our recommendations are grounded in underlying truths that will work in various situations with various people, across cultures, etc. Through these six disciplines, we intertwine research from fields as diverse as psychology, neurology, organizational behavior, project management, primary education, and personal coaching.

- Solicited feedback from PMI chapter leaders through title sponsorship of PMI's Leadership Institute Meeting for the past three years. In these conferences and meetings, our team interacts with leaders in the field of project management to stay abreast of developments on the front lines.

- Drove lively conversations with thousands of project managers across the globe through papers presented at the PMI Global Congresses in Orlando and Washington DC, global webinars, online training, and in-person training across North America.

- Conducted, and continue to conduct, interviews, surveys, and focus groups to hear directly from you and your peers. Details appear throughout the book.

- Actively collaborated across the Roeder Consulting team to build-in decades of experience on leading change. On any given day, someone on our team may point out something that science has not caught up to yet, but our experience overwhelmingly shows to be true.

Our research continues today. Each year, new scientific findings help us chip away at another little piece of the gray areas related to the human experience during times of change.

The six disciplines represent core skills that are necessary for anyone who would like to successfully lead change. They are not a formula or an algorithm. The six disciplines are a dynamic tool kit that can flex and adjust to your projects. People change. Situations change. And so must your approach.

These six disciplines may seem obvious, but they are not. Build on them. Develop them. Grow into them. You will not only become better at leading change in a project environment, but you will also become better at a wide range of human interactions.

AWARENESS

"When you are out for a walk, see to it that you watch and consider other men's postures and actions as they talk, argue, laugh, or scuffle; their own actions; and those of their supporters and onlookers."

Leonardo da Vinci

The air is thick with unpleasant smells from years of dust and who-knows-what embedded deeply into the furniture, walls, and carpeting. The client is a household name. They've been in business for generations. That fact is not surprising by the looks of this room. The depressing carpeting looks like it was installed personally by the founding father. About a dozen people are sitting around a beat-up conference table. The chairs are uncomfortable, but we're all thrilled they still work. It is my project update meeting.

My definition of success for this meeting is quite simple: Don't change my budget. Don't take away my project resources. Don't change the scope. In short, don't change anything. At the end of the hour, I am pleased. The project did not change.

Walking out of the meeting, a colleague approaches me. She was in the meeting too.

"How do you think the meeting went?" she asks.

"Great," I reply. "Nothing changed."

I ask her what she thought about the meeting.

"Well, it is clear the vice president wants the project to fail," she replies.

"What?" I ask. "He did not say that."

"Of course not, but consider this …"

She proceeds to go through a list of behaviors she observed in the meeting. Did I notice the vice president's facial expressions? I did not. Did I notice how the vice president reacted to certain comments from the main project sponsor? I did not. Did I notice this? Did I notice that? I did not … I did not … *I did not!*

That day was one of the more memorable events in my career. It clearly demonstrated to me that I had a blind spot. There was an entire aspect of managing projects that was not even on my radar screen. I was not *aware* of key signals that should have told me my project was in trouble. I needed better awareness. If *you* want to successfully lead change in your organization, so do you.

Awareness is the foundational skill for everything else related to A Sixth Sense for Project Management®. Earning buy-in, and team building are just several examples of skills that require awareness. In this chapter, I will explain the three types of awareness: self-awareness, awareness of others, and situational awareness.

The topic of awareness is a little bit "out there" for some people. Just the word itself sounds like something that is, frankly, soft. Some might ask, "How can awareness help me deliver project results?" or "Why should I care about awareness?" I have two goals in this chapter. First,

I will attempt to convince you that awareness is not only important, but in fact it is the single most important skill any project manager can possess. Second, I will share specific steps you can take to improve your awareness. No matter where you're starting point is, novice or super aware, there is always room for improvement. The exercises at the end of the chapter will help you take your awareness to the next level.

Awareness Is the Cornerstone

Consider the story at the beginning of the chapter. I was in an update meeting for a project. My job, I thought, was to manage all the stakeholders through the meeting in a way that would minimize or eliminate any need for changes. I had a detailed work plan, resources, and a scope that had been previously agreed to. Now, I just wanted to do it. Do you ever want to be isolated from everything else that is going on in your organization and just be given the space to get your work done?

In the end, the project was killed. Had I done my job as a project manager? Could I say the project was killed due to forces out of my control? Many of us may want to absolve ourselves of any responsibility. However, that is not our mission. As I argued in section one, our mission as project managers is to deliver results. We either deliver results or we don't. It's just that simple. In this case, I did not. The project failed.

What is the one thing that might have helped me save this project? Could I have saved it if I had taken another course on creating a work breakdown structure? Could I have saved the project if I put the charter in a better template? No. The death of the project had nothing to do with the work breakdown structure or any other technical skill.

The one thing I could have done was be more aware. If I had been more aware of what was going on in that room, I might have been able to channel the negative energy in some positive way. Perhaps I could have adjusted the project scope to something that was acceptable to everyone. I might have been able to eliminate a goal that was objectionable to some people, yet move on to implementation with everything else. The skill that would have enabled this is *awareness.*

Webster's Dictionary defines *aware* as "knowing; realizing; conscious." Think about one of the projects you are involved with. Can you be *more knowing, better at realizing* what is happening, and more *fully conscious* of the stakeholder expectations and requirements?

The simple truth is that awareness is the foundational skill that we must possess if we are to succeed.

Self-Awareness

Awareness starts on the inside. Self-awareness involves knowing what our strengths and weaknesses are. What are we good at? What do we like to do? What do we believe to be true? The first step to greater self-awareness is to take an inventory of our attitudes, beliefs, and capabilities.

The second step is to evaluate how each of these attitudes, beliefs, and capabilities might change based on our mood, how well rested we are or even what we had to eat for lunch. Environmental factors, such as stress, influence who we are. Perhaps we become more nervous when we are presenting to a group. That nervousness may cause us to be less competent at thinking on our feet. Typically, people perform better under some stress. A certain amount of stress energizes us, wakes us up, and makes us want to do our best. However, at some point the stress becomes too great. When we get past this breaking point, our performance deteriorates rapidly. Knowing where our personal breaking point lies is part of self-awareness.

Self-awareness can point you toward specific actions you can take to improve performance. If you become nervous while presenting, as in the example above, then you can work on your presentation skills. You can, for example, begin with presentations to a small group of friends. As you become comfortable presenting to small groups of friends you can move on to larger groups that may include some people with a different perspective than yours.

Over time, you will become less nervous and better able to think

when you present. In the short term, you might ask someone else to present so you can keep your wits about you for the critical questions stakeholders are likely to ask in the meeting. Self-awareness is a guide to help you know how to adapt to the situation, people, and environment.

Self-awareness may bring along with it some uncomfortable findings. That's okay. Keep a positive attitude and a feeling that you can overcome weaknesses. There are many cases of people overcoming situations that may have been huge obstacles to their professional success. Reportedly, Chuck Yeager became airsick the first several times he flew in an airplane. A large component of airsickness is psychological. Once he became a bit more comfortable in the plane, he had no further problems. The same is true for your interpersonal behavior in the project environment. If you constantly tell yourself you do not have good people skills, then it will be true.

A fascinating body of research shows us that "thoughts are things." In other words, you can think certain things into reality. You can visualize yourself delivering a great speech on the podium. Simply by visualizing yourself having that success, you are already starting to lay the groundwork to make that happen. Like anything, there are limits to this. You might be able to visualize yourself slam dunking a basketball. That does not necessarily mean you will be able to do an aerial 360-degree dunk with a take-off from the free-throw line the next time you're on the basketball court. *Think about your thoughts* and see if you can adjust some of your mental programming. Use self-awareness as your guide toward deeper understanding and deeper capabilities.

Awareness of Other People

Awareness can move from the inside out when you are ready. Many of the items on the project failure list are there because the project manager was not aware of other people. Consider specification requirements. Inadequate specification requirements consistently show up as one of the top reasons for project failure. Part of the reason for the failure may be traceable to the technical skill of documenting specifications. However, in many cases the failure is also the result of poor awareness. Awareness is the skill we use to understand who should be involved in creating specifications and how deep we need to go with each person to make sure we have captured all of the specifications. Awareness also tells us when something might have changed that could result in a change to specifications. Perhaps a new competitor has entered the market. You are aware of this competitor and understand that your organization may need to adjust its systems to better compete. This is less about the technical aspect of documenting and organizing requirements and more about knowing when to get requirements, who will complete the requirement, and how to complete each requirement.

Awareness of other people comes from an observation of what they say (verbal) and how they say it (nonverbal). Think about a typical debrief from a team meeting. Let's say it goes something like this …

Project manager: "I can't believe Bob said we are on the right track."
Team member: "Yes, he has been resisting this project for a long time."
Project manager: "And he said his resources are at our disposal."
Team member: "That's when Rita in HR said she has an extra resource too."
Project manager: "We are in great shape with this project!"

This conversation is a recount of the *verbal* behavior of the stakeholders in the team meeting. However, the majority of communication is nonverbal. A UCLA study determined that fully 93 percent of all communication is nonverbal. Consider how the above conversation might be different if the project manager and the teammate focus on the 93 percent of the meeting communication that came from nonverbal instead of the 7 percent that comes from the words …

Project manager: "Did Bob look more fidgety than usual?"
Team member: "Yes, why do you think that is?"
Project manager: "I'm not sure."
Team member: "Rita seemed to have a hard time looking me in the eye."
Project manager: "I guess they were just having a bad day. They're both under a lot of pressure."

With a focus on nonverbal behavior, the same meeting has now taken on a very different meaning. Let's replay the encounter one more time. This time the project manager and teammate will combine both verbal *and* nonverbal into one conversation …

Project manager: "Did Bob look a little more fidgety than usual?"
Team member: "Yes, why do you think that is?"
Project manager: "Well, he looked particularly nervous when he said his resources were at our disposal. Do you think something else is going on?"
Team member: "Maybe, because Rita looked the other way when she mumbled something about having access to one of her resources too."
Project manager: "We better look into this …"

Reconciling *what* people say with *how* they say it is a tremendously powerful way to become aware. In the third version of the conversation, we have a better understanding of the situation than we do in either of the prior two versions.

Let's dive deeper into nonverbal behavior. Nonverbal communication includes, but is not limited to the following characteristics:

- Facial expressions
- Arm positions and movements
- Head positions
- Hand movements
- Foot movements
- Eye contact/avoidance
- Posture
- Tone of voice

Each of these nonverbal cues can tell you something about a person. In Roeder Consulting's buy-in class, we divide students into three groups. We ask the first group to identify verbal and nonverbal cues of someone who is supportive of the project. The second group identifies verbal and nonverbal movements for someone who is unsure. And the third group identifies actions for a person who is resisting. After each group makes a list of these behaviors, we share them with the entire class.

Inevitably, some of the exact same behaviors show up on the list for unsure, support, and resist. For example, the behavior of "sitting motionless" sometimes shows up as a person who is unsure (the "unsure" group argues the person is sitting quietly while trying to figure out what is going on), a person who is a resister (the "resister" group argues the person is sitting stone-faced out of frustration), or a person who is supportive (the "supportive" group argues the person is listening intently and actively engaged in the project).

Another behavior the class often mentions is "frequently asking questions." Sometimes people think this behavior is a sign of resistance. In other cases, people say it is a sign of interest and support. Or it could be a sign that the person is unsure because he or she is just asking a lot of questions to understand what is going on. Either way, as you think about many of the verbal and nonverbal behaviors, it is often difficult to determine if the person is signaling support, resistance, or uncertainty.

The main point is to be careful with how you interpret nonverbal communications. Look holistically at the overall verbal and nonverbal communication experience. Constantly ask yourself if you truly understand the other person's intent, or if something is getting lost in translation. So many of the project problems I have seen have been the result of nothing more than simple miscommunication and an overall lack of awareness on the part of one or both parties.

Situational Awareness

A golf ball screams out of the tee box. The man who hit the ball is large, strong, and apparently not very accurate with his driver on this day. The ball heads directly toward a gray-haired man far down the fairway. A scream of "Fore!" comes from the tee box. It is a golfer's way of saying "dive for cover!" The gray-haired man turns calmly but rapidly surmises the situation and smoothly performs a cat-like move to shift his body out of the way. Seconds later, the ball flies through the space previously occupied by his body. Disaster had been averted.

Others may have panicked in this situation or simply put their hands over their head only to be hit. How did this man calmly and quickly assess the situation and get out of the way?

The man is Dr. Louis Csoka (pronounced *choke-ah),* an expert on situational awareness. I met Dr. Csoka at the NeuroLeadership Conference in Italy and later asked him to present at a Roeder Consulting class. This story recounts a time when he used his expert training in situational awareness to avoid injury. Dr. Csoka is a retired colonel with the United States Army. A decorated veteran from the Vietnam War, Dr. Csoka learned that awareness was a critical skill to staying alive in the battlefield. He thought that awareness was so important that he returned to West Point after his deployment and created the US Army's first performance enhancement center. Now, Dr. Csoka runs a business called Apex Performance in Charlotte, North Carolina. When you walk into Dr. Csoka's offices, you turn down a hallway and then enter a training room filled with a variety of devices. His top-end program trains executives, professional athletes, elite military forces, and others to improve their awareness and deliver peak performance. There are electrodes in the room to give participants real-time feedback. Using feedback from these sensors, people become more sensitive to their bodies' reactions to a variety of situations over time. This awareness helps them improve their ability to control those reactions.

For example, there is a pod where different sounds can be pumped in, either to activate or to relax, to create a simulated "environment." A field-goal kicker for a National Football League team may sit in this pod. Crowd noise is piped through the sound system. On the screen, the kicker can see a real-time line showing his emotional and physiological responses as he vividly visualizes his kicks. By getting this feedback, he can learn to control these responses in order to maintain a calm and focused state so essential for field-goal kickers. Through breathing exercises and mind control, he is able to move the lines. This is how technology has helped us improve our awareness and our self-regulation. Amazing technologies like this are increasingly available. Although still very expensive and out of reach for the majority of the population, this technology is teaching us more about who we are and what we are able to do to control ourselves.

Oh, and the golfing story? Dr. Csoka says there was nothing magical about it at all. "I turned and saw the ball," he recalls. "It was coming in slow motion and it appeared very large in my vision. It was easy to shift my position to avoid it. When I heard the shout 'Fore!' I responded instinctively. There has been training for this kind of reaction. It's what you develop when you train deliberately in some of the peak performance mental skills." Wouldn't it be great to be able to see all the obstacles that are aimed at us in our daily projects? You can if you improve your situational awareness.

Situational awareness also refers to the larger context of your project. What is the culture of the organization? What is going on in the company? Were layoffs recently announced? There is a good chance people will bring that stress into the project. What is the situation in the overall economy? What is going on in the world? All of these details are part of the situation. Depending on the person and the day, many of these details may affect your project environment in unexpected and difficult to decipher ways. The better you read the situation, the better you will become at knowing how to adjust to achieve project success.

Exercises to Improve Awareness

Each discipline will be followed by a section with exercises you can practice to improve your skills. It is important to note that capabilities in each discipline should be seen as a continuum. In other words, some of us may be very good at awareness, others may not pay much attention to it at all, and others still may be somewhere in between. No matter where you fit in this continuum, you can always do better.

Also, these are skills that can be developed. You may think, "Aren't some people just born with this?" Yes, some people are. However, that does not mean that the rest of us cannot take steps to improve our abilities in each of these areas. In fact, the evidence shows that many people have improved their skills in these disciplines. You can too.

Exercises to improve your awareness:

- Meeting Exercise. The next time you go into a meeting, leave time to be aware of the people in the room and the situation. Focus on verbal and nonverbal behavior of the people in the room. Do not focus only on the content of your report. It may be too difficult for you to focus both on your presentation and the people in the room. In this case, ask someone else to deliver your report while you scan the room for any details about how the people are receiving your project. This exercise will help you convert awareness into a habit. It will train you to dedicate part of your consciousness to focusing on the people and the situation while the rest of your consciousness continues to execute the work plan.

- Situational exercise. This next exercise can be done at any time in any situation. Stop and take a moment to pay attention to what all of your senses are telling you. What do you see? Do not try to interpret the information—just receive it. What do you hear? There are often louder sounds that are obvious and others that you consciously hear only after active listening. Do you taste anything? Maybe you taste a breakfast burrito that you wish you had never eaten. How about touch? What does the chair feel like? Are your clothes digging in? Does your environment have any unique smells? Finally, don't forget about your sixth sense. What is your gut telling you? Your heart? Is your body trying to send you signals right now? Do you have hunches or an intuition about your current situation? Over time, just paying attention to the situation around you will yield fresh new insights. Try it now!

- The "world is a mirror" exercise. Each time you interact with someone, he or she tells you a little something about yourself. The next time you meet with a person, let's say a key stakeholder, pay attention to what that person might be telling you about yourself. Is he or she talking to you in a condescending way? Maybe the person doesn't respect you. Does he or she look sincere and genuinely interested in your opinion? Maybe he or she sees you as a true partner.

What is the person telling you about yourself, and what are you going to do with that information?

- "The prick in your arm" exercise. Try this for an hour. Every time something occurs during that hour that is even a little bit stressful, imagine experiencing the discomfort of a prick in your arm. When that stressful event happens, no matter how small, ask yourself if there is anything you can do differently next time to avoid the stress. These mini-moments in life build on us and wear us down. Use this exercise to figure out ways to be aware of your life's stresses and minimize them. Your body will thank you.

WHOLE BODY
DECISIONS™

It is decision time. I am in a sales and marketing role for one of the world's top automobile manufacturers. I can stay on my current career path, which would probably mean a move out of state, or I can switch to a different role, which would allow me to stay put. There are many things to consider. What career options will I have with each choice? Which team will be better to work with? How long do I think I'll be with this company anyway? The decision is overwhelming.

I create a pros/cons table to help me make the decision. I sit on an outside bench with a tablet of paper and write "Pros" on the top left-hand side of the page. I diligently list all of the benefits of Option A. Then, I write "Pros" again on the top right corner. That's where all of the benefits of Option B go. Eventually I write the cons for both options on the bottom of the sheet. I stare at the sheet of paper. What's the answer? Maybe if I keep staring at it the answer will come to me. Nuts. That's what someone might remark if they happened to be watching me. I'm sitting on a park bench in a stare-down with a piece of paper. No decision is coming to me. Why isn't this working?

Next, I try talking to some people. Every time I talk to them, I discuss the details of the situation as factually as I can. I consider myself analytical, reasonable, and fact-based. I don't want emotions to get into my decision-making process. I dutifully relay the facts of each option:

> Here's what I would be doing …
> The next step in this career path would be …
> Expected income is …

And so on.

Days pass. Still, I do not have an answer. My frustration grows. I think through the facts again. Maybe I missed something? Maybe, there is a piece of information that will tip the scales toward one of the two options.

It turns out, I now understand, that I was relying entirely on a fact-based decision-making process. In addition to the facts, I should have also incorporated my heart and my gut. In many cases, particularly some of life's biggest choices, our rational decision-making processes are not enough. The solution is Whole Body Decisions.™

How Are Whole Body Decisions™ Relevant to Project Management?

Project managers constantly make decisions. These decisions make a difference. It is self-evident that we want our decisions to be good. If there was a better way to make decisions, would you be willing to learn it?

Most contemporary project management training teaches a rational, fact-based approach to the discipline. Project managers gather requirements. Requirements are facts about what the project must achieve. Project managers create a work plan populated with dates, key deliverables, and other tangible goals. Project managers use a structured process and a set of templates that we call our methodology. It is all about the facts.

Further, many professional project managers, and people in almost any other profession, have received a lifetime of education grounded almost entirely in facts and rational decisions. Did any of your academic courses teach you how to listen to your gut? Most of us would say, "No."

Consider the story of a senior manager who worked for one of my clients. "I am an engineer in training," he told me. "When it comes to change, I like to think you just put the facts out there and they speak for themselves. Now, I am learning there is a lot more to it than that." He had achieved a high level of management primarily based on his technical skills. Now, he was learning a new world. He was learning, fairly quickly I might add, the world of interpersonal skills during times of change.

Here's another example. A number of years ago, Roeder Consulting was hosting a class in an auditorium of approximately fifty people. I was standing in the aisle while one of my colleagues presented. A gentleman sitting on the aisle leaned over and whispered to me, "This is great, this people skills stuff. I'm an engineer and we're never trained on any of this." Can you relate to this engineer?

We are often misguided by the so-called "facts and data" that come from a rational thought process. These facts do not tell us how to work with people. They do not tell us the full story. We need a better way. Whole Body Decisions™ is a technique you can deploy to consistently make the very best decisions. This is done by capturing and processing all of the information available to us.

Heart, Gut, and Rational Brain

Whole Body Decisions™ is a close companion to Awareness. When you become more aware, you will also dramatically increase the amount of information flowing into your consciousness. You need a way to filter through this information. You need to determine what pieces to act on, what pieces of information to disregard, and what pieces to keep track of for potential action in the future. Whole Body Decisions™ provides the tools needed to sort through all this information. Whole Body Decisions™ is a technique to triangulate between heart, gut, and rational brain. Separately, each of these three can help us to make decisions. Together, our heart, brain, and gut form a powerful partnership of robust information and intelligence.

Heart

For centuries, people have described the heart as a source of emotions, truth, and decision-making. According to *The HeartMath Solution* by Doc Childre and Howard Martin, ancient cultures, including the Egyptians, Babylonians, and Greeks, believed that the heart was the primary organ responsible for emotions, morality, and decision-making. In contemporary culture, how often are you coached to "listen to your heart," "follow your heart," or "put your heart into it"?

Intriguingly, our science is beginning to catch up with what many have known for centuries. We now know that there are 40,000 nerve endings in the heart. The heart senses and communicates information in its own way. Research shows the heart transmits information to other areas of the human body using at least three methods: neurologically through one's nerves, chemically through hormones and neurotransmitters, and physically through pressure waves. Much of this communication serves as a source of useful information for our decisions.

Further, there is evidence the heart may communicate in a fourth way by using energy through its electromagnetic field. Our hearts, it turns out, are the strongest electromagnetic forces in our bodies. The electrical changes in feelings transmitted by our hearts can be measured eight to ten feet away using current measuring devices. There is a good chance people are able to sense these electromagnetic signals. We may literally broadcast our emotions electromagnetically to those around us, and pick up emotions from the electromagnetic heart waves of those close to us.

Clearly, the heart is a powerful source of information. Our hearts should be sitting at the table when we make decisions. However, alone this information may not be sufficient to make the best decisions. There are other pieces of information we still need to access.

Gut

Our gut is a second source of information. Dr. Michael Gershon argues in his book *The Second Brain* that our predecessors developed a gut with a mind of its own so our brain would not need to devote precious cerebral resources to functions, such as digesting food. In common culture we often make comments like, "I just had a gut feeling" or "follow your gut."

Our gut, defined as the small intestine, esophagus, stomach, and large intestine, has more nerve endings than our spine. There are 100 million nerve endings in the small intestine alone. Nerve cells communicate with each other and with other cells using neurotransmitters. According to Dr. Gershon, all of the classes of neurotransmitter that are found in the brain are also found in our gut. This suggests that our gut may rival our brain in complexity and functionality. Evidence also shows the gut can "make decisions" and take actions on its own without involvement from the brain. For example, the gut is able to activate reflexive behaviors on its own, whereas reflexive behavior in any other part of the body requires involvement of either the brain or the spinal cord.

When you stop to think about it, it should not be surprising that information is communicated to us through the gut. Do you ever get butterflies in your stomach when you are nervous? Have you felt indigestion at particularly stressful moments? This is your body, via the gut, communicating information to you. So-called "gut feelings" are not just limited to your physical midsection. Some people also report feelings in other parts of their body. A hand might start tingling or a nerve twitching under certain circumstances. The more aware we are, the better we become at knowing what that sensation means.

Clearly, in addition to the heart, the gut is also a powerful source of information for decision-making. A person's gut is an intelligent ally and should also be sitting at the table when we make decisions. However, alone this information still may not be sufficient to make the best decisions.

Rational Brain

Interestingly, our brain has not always been given proper credit for its importance. According to *Your Brain: A User's Guide* from *Time* magazine, ancient Egyptians considered the brain unimportant and discarded it during the process to mummify a corpse. Aristotle believed the brain's role was to cool heated blood from the heart. Today, the brain is considered by many people to be the most significant executive center in our body. We see this in our common language with phrases like "use your head," "think about it," and "get your head in the game."

Our brains, indeed, are very powerful tools for decision-making. Consider that 77 percent of the average human brain is made up of the cerebral cortex where higher functioning occurs. Compare this to 31 percent for a rat. Our brains have many different areas with considerable discussion on which areas control which functions. For example, there is evidence that the simple left brain / right brain dichotomy, where it is argued that each hemisphere of the brain controls certain functions, may not be as crisp as once thought. Many functions seem to involve multiple areas of the brain and can even move to a different part of the brain after injury. Our brains adapt.

When it comes to decision-making, our brains are vital. The brain is good at processing details and facts and putting them in some kind of order that makes sense. Project managers often excel at processing rational information. This is incredibly useful in many situations. In other situations, such as the career decision I needed to make in the story at the beginning of this chapter, our rational brain-based processes can leave us sorely lacking.

Each of the three sources of information I mentioned—heart, gut, and rational brain—is a formidable source of information and decision-making in its own right. Combined together they are incredibly powerful. Whole Body Decisions™ is based on the premise that the best decisions are made when as much available information as possible is captured. Therefore, the best decisions should capture information from all three of these tools: heart, gut, and rational brain.

How to Make Whole Body Decisions™

The process to make Whole Body Decisions™ is easy to understand. Simply listen to all of the available information from three sources of information: brain, heart, and gut. *How* to do that is a lifelong pursuit.

The first step is to open your mind to the reality that your brain may not have all of the answers. Some people never get past this step. For you to become proficient in Whole Body Decisions™, you must get past this step. You must be willing to accept that the brain does not always know what to do.

Next, begin to pay attention to the information from your heart and gut. It is there. However, when we focus entirely on our brain, we may disregard the others. You may have spent your entire adult life learning how to shut out anything you thought was not relevant to decision-making. Now we are going to reverse that. But we are not letting the heart and gut take over. We are simply giving them a seat at the table when decisions are made. You can choose to accept their input or not.

Become aware of how your body feels. Why does it feel a certain way? Is it what you ate for lunch or is it something you are thinking about? Is it the caffeine from your morning coffee or is it anxiety about a report that is due in two hours? Think about *how* your body feels at any point in time and *why* it might feel that way. You are starting to get conscious access to the information you will require to make Whole Body Decisions.™

Finally, close your eyes, take a few deep breaths, and clear your mind. After several moments of quiet, think about the decision you are trying to make. Pay attention to what your brain is telling you. Also, pay attention to how your gut feels. Is it telling you something? Pay attention to your heart and your emotions. How does the decision make you feel? Now you are tapping into very rich databases of information. You are making decisions with all available data. Whole Body Decisions™ is the ultimate in fact-based decision-making. Whole Body Decisions™ incorporate all of the facts, not just those from your powerful but limited rational brain.

Whole Body Decisions™ require practice and time. Do not get frustrated if it does not "work" the first time. Continue to go through these steps.

Over time, you will improve this skill. This will help you make better decisions to deliver project success. It will also help you in any area of life that requires decision-making.

Whole Body Decisions™ Exercises

Exercises to improve your ability to make Whole Body Decisions™:

- Closed-eye exercise. The next time you're faced with a decision and you don't know what the best path is, try the following. Let's say you're trying to figure out what clothes to wear to a neighbor's party. You have it narrowed down to two choices. Go through the normal rational process. For example, you might ask if it is a holiday. Is there a certain color associated with the holiday? You may rule out certain clothes because they are dirty. Go through your rational process and if you still haven't decided, try the following. Close your eyes, take a few deep breaths, and think about option number one. Pay attention to your whole body. Maybe your heart rate picks up, you begin to sweat, and you feel your fists tighten up. This awareness may be your body telling you that something about option number one is not right. Now think about option number two. Your hands become more comfortable. You feel your heart rate slow down. Your breathing slows down. Is your body telling you option number two is the better choice? You are now making Whole Body Decisions.™

- Open-eye exercise. At Roeder Consulting, we are real-world project managers. I know it is not always practical to sit at your desk, close your eyes, and reflect on decisions. The boss might think you've gone off the deep end. Discretion is the key. If you can't find privacy, then try the closed-eyed exercise at home. Over time, you will become better at processing all of the information available to you without shutting down visual input. Then you can make Whole Body Decisions™ with open eyes at work too.

- Learn about your gut. Developing Whole Body Decisions™ requires simultaneously improving your awareness skills at each of the three sources of information: heart, gut, and brain. Here is an exercise you can perform to improve your sensitivity to gut. The next time you feel discomfort in your gut, ask yourself what you were thinking about at the very moment you felt that twinge of discomfort. Also, recall what you were doing. What actions were you taking at that very moment? Over time, you will begin to pinpoint certain thoughts and actions that trigger discomfort in your gut. It is fascinating and very informative to your self-awareness.

- Listen to your heart. We often connect our heart to emotions. In this exercise, allow yourself to listen to the emotions you associate to a particular event. Let's say a project meeting is scheduled for tomorrow. Further, let's say these meetings always make you tense. Allow yourself to think about the emotions of the meeting. What exactly is creating stress within you? Do not pass judgment on the emotions. Listen to them and accept them. When you are done, write down the items that created stress. Think about ways to mitigate them just as you would mitigate any other risk in your project. This exercise will improve your ability to listen to your heart.

Chapter 6

CLEAR COMMUNICATION

*"The single biggest problem in communication
is the illusion that it has taken place."*

George Bernard Shaw

You can hear the anger in his voice. There is no mistaking that he is upset. Why? We asked him about this very issue just days ago. He told us he supported the idea. Now, we're on a conference call with some other important people and he is confrontational. He could not be more disagreeable if he tried. Why? Moments like this make me wonder why I didn't become an airline pilot or a park ranger. Anything but a project manager ...

After the conference call ends in flames, I reflect on the carnage. What happened? Where did we go wrong? How did yesterday's support turn into today's venomous anger? The angry man is the vice president of marketing for the main division of a highly successful Fortune 500 company. I'll call him Robert. Days ago, we had "pre-presented" our team's recommendations to Robert. One of the recommendations was the following:

> *Several people from Robert's organization will report into a newly formed group.*

Robert supported this recommendation. He told us the people in question had skills that were more closely aligned to the new group than to his marketing group. Robert has more than one hundred people in his organization. The transition of several folks, he said, would not make a big difference to the marketing group. Robert was confident his team could still achieve its goals for the current fiscal year.

Then, in this meeting today, we get into a conference call to make a final decision with the larger group of stakeholders. That's the meeting I described in the opening paragraph. In that meeting, we present our recommendation …

> *Several people from Robert's organization will report into a newly formed group.*

It's exactly what Robert already agreed to. It is stated exactly the same way. Why did Robert appear to change his mind? As the team and I reflect on his apparent "about-face," we decide the best course of action is to "run to the problem." We schedule a follow-up call with Robert.

We get into the call and immediately the conversation accelerates to the heart of the matter. Robert says he can't understand why we think his organization will report into the newly formed group. Marketing is responsible for all kinds of activities, Robert says, that have nothing to do with this new group. Why do we think, Robert asks us, his entire group should report into the new group?

Now, I'm starting to figure out what happened. Remember what Robert agreed to and what we restated in the stakeholder meeting? Here it is again:

> *Several people from Robert's organization will report into a newly formed group.*

When we had our initial meeting with Robert, he heard the full statement and agreed with it. For whatever reasons—maybe there was a glitch in the phone line or maybe his assistant put a note on his desk distracting him as we were talking—when we presented it to the larger stakeholder group, *he did not hear the first three words* of the recommendation. In other words, instead of hearing "Several people from Robert's organization will report into a newly formed group," Robert heard, "Robert's organization will report into a newly formed group."

No wonder he was so upset on the stakeholder call. He thought we had suddenly decided the entire marketing group should report into the new group.

We quickly cleared the air and fixed the misunderstanding. I was left with a deeper appreciation of how easily communications can go wrong. Project managers must be expert communicators to successfully lead change.

Barriers to Clear Communication

When I talk about communication in this book, what I mean specifically is the following: is the idea that is in my head the same as the idea that is in your head? If it is the same, I have clearly communicated. The following communication model shows the complexity involved with simply getting ideas from our heads into other people's heads.

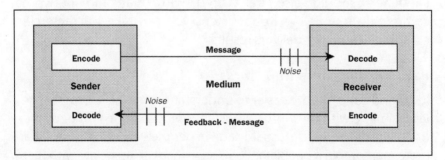

Exhibit 6-1 Basic Communication Model from PMBOK® Guide

Start at the top left. When you create a message and send it to someone else, there is interference between the two of you. This could be noise in the phone line, distractions that occur during the communication, or any other variety of issues. On the top right, some portion of the message you initially send arrives in the receiver's brain. Now the receiver will send this message through his or her own filters to try to make sense of it. The receiver may twist and adjust your message into a format more comfortable to him or her. When the receiver has decoded the message, he or she will then process it and send you a return message. This return message is now subject to all of the "noise" and barriers of the external environment. Cultural, language, and generational differences can manifest themselves in the improper encoding of your message to the receiver *and* in the decoding and encoding in the receiver's head. The receiver may select words that mean something different to you than what is intended. When you add it all up, there are multiple opportunities for the message to be changed and misinterpreted.

This simple chart gives us an appreciation for just how difficult it is to transfer messages. So what are the actions we can take to minimize this confusion? We can start by using powerful language that leaves less room for interpretation.

Tips for Clear Communication

Clear communication is facilitated by language that is understandable. Language should also be paired with matching nonverbal communication. Below, I detail steps you can take to create clear communication that delivers results.

Paint Visual Pictures with Words

Ideas and concepts are easier to understand if people can associate a visual image with the words. Make your presentation come to life by using words to create a visual image in people's minds. Also, ideas are more memorable if people have a visual image to associate with them. You are engaging a different part of their whole body with visual imagery, making them more likely to understand and remember.

Be Careful with Clichés, Jargon, Catch Phrases, and Acronyms

Words and phrases outside common language may mean something to you. However, other people may not understand them. Even worse, other people may have another interpretation that is less friendly. Remember, the point of communication is to get ideas from your head into other people's heads. If they do not understand what you are saying, then you have failed to communicate.

I once worked with an executive who fought acronyms in any sort of document. Her organization, it seemed, had an acronym for just about everything. She made sure that acronyms did not show up in written documents. She required everything to be spelled out.

Clear Nonverbal Communication

Nonverbal communication is also important to being clear. Your nonverbal communication should not be distracting and should match what you are saying. For example, if you smile when you deliver bad news, this will create confusion. People may wonder if you are happy about the bad news. Constantly remind yourself to align nonverbal messages with verbal messages.

What to Communicate When

I would like to address one aspect of communication that I learned through experience on many projects. I have not seen this addressed in any other communication course, yet I have found it to be one of the most useful attributes of delivering project results. It has to do with *what* to communicate *when*.

First, I'd like to share a story of "what to communicate when" gone awry. I am working at a Fortune 500 client on a major project that is creating a new field organization. One of the items the project team must define is the number of people who are required to be in this new organization. As typically happens in the process, we go through a lot of variability in this number. The chart below shows the sort of churn we went through as part of the normal process.

Getting to the Answer

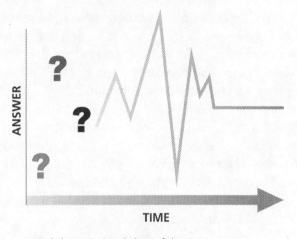

Exhibit 6-2 Variability of the Answer over
a Typical Consulting Engagement

Initially we thought the number of people in the group would be fairly low. Then someone pointed out a new responsibility the group would have that was not included in our calculations. This new responsibility would take a lot of time. We needed more people, so the forecasted number of people in the field went up. Then a new efficiency improvement was identified. The number went back down. All of this was a normal part of our due diligence as we worked through all available information.

The problem occurred when one of the people on our team, I'll call her Jane, communicated these changes to the would-be manager of the new group. With all the best intentions, Jane went to the group manager and said something like, "Tough news. The group is going to be very small. We'll need to find new roles for many of the people we were planning to put into this position." A week or so later, when our model said the number would be high, Jane went back to the manager saying something like, "Well, now the number of people in the new group will be very high. We're going to need to staff up! Better start recruiting!" The next week Jane was back with a message that the number had gone back down. Again, Jane had the best intentions. She wanted to give the new manager a "heads-up" so he could get ready for the changes. Instead, she inadvertently confused the person while discrediting the team. The manager asked why the team's number kept changing. He said, "Doesn't the team know what it is doing?"

What could we do differently in this situation? I talked to Jane as I observed this happening. She felt it was her duty to let this person know what was going on as quickly as possible. I spent time thinking through what was happening. I sketched a rough version of the following chart on a sheet of paper:

What to Communicate When

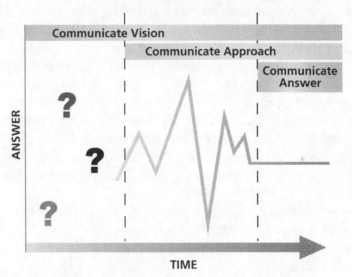

Exhibit 6-3 What to Communicate When

A few days later, I shared the chart with some people on the project team. They liked it. I knew I was onto something. Since then I have used it regularly and we teach it in our program on executing strategy.

I will discuss what this chart shows. In the early days of a strategic project, we typically are not in a position to predict what the final answers will be. Obviously, we are not in a position to communicate answers when we don't have them. However, that does not mean we should not communicate anything. Individuals fill in communication voids with their own version of what might be going on. This type of back-channel misinformation can create chaos on your project. So we always want to communicate something. In the early days, that "something" should be the overall vision and goals. Tell people what the project is about and why you're doing it. What business objective (think business acumen) will this project help achieve?

As the project progresses, you will begin to have more clarity on *how* you are going to answer the key questions. You will create some sort of methodology that will be consistently applied to the question(s) at hand. Meet with people and share your approach. Invite them to refine the approach. Ask if you have the right attributes in the model or approach. What would they add? What do they have questions about? When you are comfortable with the approach and/or decision model, communicate it to the broader group of stakeholders. You still do not have answers, but you are letting them know how you will get them. If you think it is appropriate, invite the larger group to provide feedback on the methodology. You are achieving two goals here. First, you are getting excellent input on the approach to help ensure it is the best it can be. Second, you are starting to gain support. You will communicate results at a later date in the project. When you do, you can gently remind people that they were involved in the process that led to the results. They themselves thought it was a good process.

Finally, you communicate the results. This happens only after you get to the flat line in the exhibit. Do not communicate results until the team's analysis is complete and you are confident you have arrived at the best answer.

Look at the chart again and notice the overlap in the three communication phases. Vision may be helpful to communicate even after you have started to talk about methodology. In fact, you may want to communicate vision during the entire length of the project. It is helpful to constantly remind people *why* you are doing what you're doing. Also, when you begin to communicate results you will want to start by reminding people of the methodology you used to get there.

Simplify the Complex

When I was in business school, a professor of organizational behavior showed us a video of the CEO of a Fortune 500 company. When the video began, the first thing you saw was a well-dressed, sophisticated, intelligent-looking man. He began to talk, and his sentence structure was just right. He used many big words that clearly had been carefully chosen. From a grammatical standpoint, there was not a single thing wrong with his delivery. At the end of his two-minute speech, the professor turned off the video. She asked us what he had just said. We were able to remember some specific bits and pieces. "What is his overall message?" she asked. We did not know. "What should you do with this information?" We could not answer that. As she pressed us more, it turned out that we had absolutely no idea what the man had just said. We understood the words. But put together it was mumbo-jumbo. The moral of the story was that the man spent a very brief period of time in the CEO role. He clearly was smart, but he did not know how to boil down his message to a few key points.

Clear communication is about making sure people know what you are saying. Use simple language. Figure out a way to make the complex simple. In fact, that is what some say is the most important aspect of great communicators and leaders—the ability to make the complex simple. If you are in doubt, try the "eighth-grader" test. Most of the newspapers in the United States are written for people with an eighth-grade reading level. If you present to an eighth-grader, will he or she know what you were talking about? Are your choice of words, sentence structure, and overall messaging clear?

Of course, you can adjust this if you are speaking to a conference of people who all work in your field. Any professional speaker will tell you it is important to know your audience. It is always best, though, to err on the side of simplicity.

Virtual Teams

Increasingly, project teams are getting some or all of their work done in a virtual environment. As more technology becomes available to facilitate virtual communications, cost and timeline pressures will continue this trend.

Difficult communication issues become even more complex in a virtual team environment. Consider that most communication is nonverbal as discussed in the prior section. A large portion of this nonverbal communication is lost in a virtual environment. However, all nonverbal communication is not lost.

Research shows that in-person communication is best for building relationships and trust. A video teleconference is the next best option. In a video teleconference, you can see some nonverbal behavior of those you are meeting with. Until recently, video teleconferencing was very expensive and also very difficult to use. I recall one of my clients showing me a large room filled with state-of-the art technology for virtual communications. He said it was almost as if the person was sitting next to you. I asked him how often his company used it. "Never," he replied, "It's too complicated." Another client told me he needs a group of engineers to figure out how to get their virtual technology room up and running.

However, there are now Internet-based packages that offer live-streaming video and audio. If possible, take advantage of this type of technology for virtual meetings. If you can see each other, you are going to provide and receive more nonverbal information, which will ease communication.

If you are limited to a telephone, it is still possible to capture some nonverbal information. For example, pay attention to tone of voice and rate of speech. If tone and rate change during the conversation, it may be an indication of the person's attitudes toward your project.

The least effective method for virtual communication is e-mail. Studies show it is difficult to build trust using e-mail. It seems people just do not have the same connection to you with e-mail, and a person's choice of words can often be misconstrued. Even worse, research from the University of Illinois shows people are less likely to be honest when using e-mail.

Which of the following is your preferred mode of workplace communication?

ANSWERS	PERCENTAGES
Email	49%
Doorway (face to face, one on one)	30%
Phone call	5%
Internet video conferencing	2%
Post-it note (or something actually written on actual paper)	0%
No Answer	14%

Exhibit 6-4 Communication Preferences

Regrettably, a lot of project work is conducted using email. Consider the above survey results from one of Roeder Consulting's recent webinars. Forty-nine percent of the audience preferred email to any other form of communication. As a profession, we should re-consider our reliance on this tool. An in-person meeting or a video teleconference is a much better way to facilitate clear communication.

Meet Before Going Virtual

If possible, conduct an in-person meeting when you launch major projects. In-person meetings require extra budget and extra planning. However, the benefits of having everyone together in person are tremendous. Use the in-person meeting as an opportunity to achieve the dual goals of conducting business and building the team.

Conduct Business

The first meeting is a chance to review the charter with everyone. Ensure that the full team is moving in the right direction. Use it as a chance to get feedback on the project scope if you are in a position to adjust the scope. Begin to delegate work tasks and make sure everyone leaves the meeting with something specific to do.

Build the Team

Schedule generous amounts of time for team building. Give everyone an opportunity to get to know one another. Round-robin icebreakers, where each person is forced to talk to every other person, are very effective if the team is twenty people or smaller. Also, have a team lunch or dinner while everyone is in town. Get to know people outside the normal work environment. This type of bonding will deliver tremendous dividends later in the project.

After the first in-person meeting, you can consider switching to a virtual setting. When people are on the phone, they will have some context to build from. Let's say one person sounds gruff on the phone. If you have met him in person, you will know that his voice always sounds that way, but everything else about him is positive.

Virtual meetings can carry the team for a period of time but not indefinitely. At some point, the latency of the in-person meeting is lost. At that point, bring people back together to reconnect and rebuild relationships. Earlier this year, I was interviewed for a newspaper article discussing recent research from executive leadership professor Gregory Northcraft of the University of Illinois. In an executive summary of his research, Professor Northcraft stated, "My parents live in North Carolina and even though I e-mail them a lot, that's not good enough. I need to visit and recharge that relationship every once in a while so we still feel connected." I told the reporter this research was consistent with my experience leading projects. Teams operate more smoothly if there are occasionally in-person meetings.

Don't Let the Technology Get in the Way

If you are using virtual technology, set aside part of the first meeting to train everyone how to use the technology. Explain how the audio will work. Show them the different screens and windows. Ask them to practice sharing documents. This increases in importance as you bring people onto the team who are not part of your organization. People in your organization, with luck, use the same technology for meetings. However, outside people may have never used your technology platform. If they spend their time on the call trying to figure out how to see the video screen of you, then you can bet they are not going to do a great job processing whatever points you are trying to make.

If you are using a phone line only, start with a voice check. Have each person say hello or identify himself or herself to confirm that you can hear each other. Also, this will enable others on the phone to associate a voice with a name. Some people may say, "This is Tres ..." before beginning their statement. It is not a bad idea for groups that do not know each other well. However, I have seen it get out of control when there are relatively few people and one person announces herself every time well after everyone else knows who she is.

Meet People One-on-One

Before any group meeting, whether in-person or virtual, it is best to get to know each team member or stakeholder in a one-on-one environment. If possible, do not allow your first major meeting with the team to be in a large group conversation. Get to know each person in a one-on-one setting. Schedule a phone call. When you talk to the person, you will get a better understanding of who he is. E-mail is only written words. No voice tone. Talking to someone on the phone offers a more robust database of personal information. You can hear tone of voice. This could give some hypothesis about the person's outlook. Does she sound upbeat and positive? Also, in a phone conversation you may get into sidebars where you get to know each other better. You may talk about family. You may discuss a recent sporting event or a current event in the news. This establishes connections and provides some context to get to know the person.

It is important to have this initial contact one-on-one for two main reasons. First, you can focus all of your attention on getting to know one person at a time. You do not need to manage group dynamics. Second, people often act differently in group situations. You'll first want to get to know them as individuals. Then, when you observe them in a group setting, you'll expand your awareness. If their behavior changes dramatically, you will want to note that. Do certain people in the group tend to cause them to talk more or less? Do they tend to agree more with some people than with others? All of this should go into your mental map of the human side of your project.

Simplicity in Virtual Meetings

Simplifying the complex is even more important in a virtual setting. Consider how difficult it is to communicate a key point in a conference room where everyone is sitting in front of you. Of course, all of that difficulty is present in a virtual meeting too. Now consider that a virtual meeting adds additional obstacles. They may not see you. They may have a difficult time hearing you. Many conference-calling bridges experience a situation where different people are at different volumes. You may need to turn the volume all the way up for Joe in Des Moines. But when Jorge from Spain begins to speak, it nearly blasts out your eardrums. Have you ever sat on a conference call with your finger on the volume button adjusting up and down for each speaker? It's the new office sport.

This is just one example of the numerous technology snafus that can add challenges upon challenges in a virtual environment. Language barriers may also occur. Of course, we all know that conducting business across countries and continents brings new challenges as we work to understand different languages, cultures, and norms. However, this phenomenon is not limited to international calls. As Roeder Consulting delivers classes across different cities in North America, we have found different geographic norms as well. These different norms can lead to misunderstandings. If you have people on the phone who do not work for your company, this further amplifies the difficulties. Vendors, consultants, and customers are just a few examples of groups who may be involved in team meetings. They might have different norms and expectations than you.

In summary, pay attention to whether your message is being heard and understood. Tell stories, use clear and direct language, and provide proper time for people to play back what they heard. When meeting virtually, select a technology with maximum interactivity. Live streaming video is best. Overall, always exercise awareness to make sure your messages are clear, and also use awareness to have reasonable assurances that you are properly interpreting what others are trying to communicate to you.

Clear Communication Exercises

Exercises to improve your Clear Communication:

- "Change the channel" exercise. Think about a person on your project team who does not seem to understand the team's goal even after multiple communications. Try a different communication channel. Different people process information in different ways. Let's say you have sent her an e-mail five times and she keeps asking you questions that are clearly answered in the e-mail. Some people are visual; they might want to see a chart, so try sending that person a chart. Other people are verbal and will do much better from a conversation. If you're in an environment where you can do so, walk down the hallway and sit in front of her. If you're in a virtual environment, call her on the phone. Figure out some other way to communicate your message to her.

- "Cut out the middle person" exercise. Did you play the "telephone" game in elementary school where everyone stands in a semicircle and forwards a message to the person next to him or her? The teacher begins a message at one end the semicircle. Then each person, in turn, repeats the message to the person next to him or her. By the time the message gets to the end of the line, it is completely different from the original message. Well, this happens in our projects every day. You provide direction to someone who, in turn, communicates it to someone else and so on. By the time your message gets to the final person, the message may be very different from the one you intended. If you are having communication problems in your project, try to cut out as many of the middle people as possible. Reach out directly to people deep into your project and ensure they have the right message.

- "Test the copy" exercise. Almost every week, I gain new appreciation for a word or phrase that means one thing to me and something different to other people. For example, in one of our classes we discuss a leader who says he will use a "bottom-up approach." To me, that term means that he will talk with people at lower levels in the organization chart, solicit their input, and use it to inform his decisions. To other people in the class, "bottom-up approach" is more process-based. They think it means the leader will look at the details of the organization's processes and manage accordingly. What words and terms are you using today that others interpret differently? In this exercise, take copy from an important project document, such as a charter or a definition of scope. Test the copy with a few people. Does it mean to them what it means to you? Make adjustments as necessary to ensure everyone is in agreement.

- "I want to make sure I understand" exercise. This is a reversal of the prior exercise. What are you missing? Think about a key piece of information related to the project. Are you fully grasping the intent? Are you interpreting the words differently than someone else? Go to the author of the document and say, "I want to make sure I understand. Can you explain to me more detail on ...?" Early in my consulting career, I worked on projects with a senior partner who was considered, by many, to be brilliant. I watched him in a number of cases ask what many might have called a "stupid question." He just kept asking and asking until he was 100 percent sure he got it. He did it with confidence and he got to the bottom of the issue. His questions not only ensured he had the right idea in his head, but did the same for the other people in the room too. Watching him instilled in me the importance of asking as many questions as necessary until it is clear everyone in the meeting understands.

ADAPTABILITY

*"It ain't what you don't know that gets you into trouble.
It's what you know for sure that just ain't so."*

Mark Twain

I am sitting in the corporate office of a consumer-products company based in Winston-Salem, North Carolina. The office has a safari theme. When you enter the front door, you are greeted by wall coverings, art, and other effects that give the feeling of being on a safari. It is an appropriate theme because at the moment I feel like I am stranded in the Serengeti. The work plan in front of me has grown into a monstrosity. We are using one of the traditional project-management software tools to map out our plan. My client is launching a new business unit. This business unit has less than one year to design, manufacture, and launch a new product line. The marching orders from the chief executive officer are to make the business unit profitable its first year in operation. This is a tall order because new ventures often take years to achieve profitability.

For the last several weeks, I have been working with the division president, the vice president of marketing, and other key people to create a work plan for the product launch. Each person has contributed his or her input into the work plan. They shared what needs to be done, what the dependencies are, how long it will take, etc. Instead of bringing clarity to the project, it has brought us to a grinding halt. I am staring at a work plan gone haywire. What to do? I am a project manager. I'm supposed to use project management software, right?

I meet with the vice president of marketing to discuss the dilemma. Both of us have arrived at the same conclusion. The work plan is helpful as a tool to manage certain aspects of the product launch. However, as a plan for the overall launch of the new division, the software tool is just too cumbersome and not able to keep up with all of the daily variability without an overwhelming amount of effort. It is hindering instead of helping. We ditch the software for the full project, but keep it for the product design, development, and launch. In short, we adapted.

One year later, I talk with the division president. "How did we do?" I ask. He replies that we did a great job. The product launched and the division was profitable in year one. They changed successfully.

We Succeed When We Adapt

In 2008, the Project Management Institute published a multiyear, almost $2.5 million project titled *Researching the Value of Project Management*. The study's goal was to answer the following questions: Does project management deliver value? And if it does, what are the key drivers of project value? Not surprisingly, this study showed that project management does deliver value.

However, this research also showed that project management does not always deliver value. In fact, in some cases, the discipline of project management makes things worse. We make things worse when we fail to adapt our project management approach and methodologies to the situation. In other words, if we take the same methodologies, the same tools, the same processes and apply them like peanut butter across every project, every situation, every size of organization, and every culture, then the odds are we will destroy value in some cases. As a profession, we need to learn how to adapt to our environment.

Researching the Value of Project Management also found that firms that conduct more than the average amount of training on people skills are more likely to have projects that deliver value. The researchers conducted sixty case studies around the globe and found that organizations that train their people *more* than average on people skills are more likely to have projects that deliver value.

I met Mark Mullaly, one of the coauthors of *Researching the Value of Project Management*, in 2008 when Roeder Consulting sponsored his keynote address at the Leadership Institute Meeting in Denver, Colorado. My review of his book gave me a strong impression that the research had determined people skills are very important. Mark, a tall man with red hair and a goatee, corroborated this perspective with the following note to me: "Certainly, in our findings, the ability of project managers [to] engage in critical thinking skills, to understand the business, and to respond in ways that are situationally appropriate are critical to those organizations that are realizing significant value."

Chameleon with a Core™

Successful project managers adapt their approach to the conditions of the environment. You may have noticed by now that each of the disciplines has a graphic image associated with it. These images appear at the beginning of each chapter in section two. They have been professionally designed to reflect each discipline. The adaptability image is a chameleon. A chameleon changes its skin color to the environment around it. This provides the chameleon with camouflage and an extra level of security. Project managers, as clearly documented in *Researching the Value of Project Management*, must learn to adapt to the environment.

One area where this is particularly important is in our project management methodology. There are many different methodologies one can use to manage a project. There is a hot debate in our profession about which methodology is the best. Research indicates that the answer is, "It depends." There is not a single methodology that works best in all situations. So one basic area where project managers need to adapt is in the selection of the methodology that is best for the particular project at hand. Perhaps you work in an organization with a completely standardized approach to managing projects. In this case, there may still be actions you can take to "semi-customize" your approach to the particular project you are working on. Maybe you don't need to follow every single step in the process. Maybe you can add an additional process if the standard approach does not include it. The important take-away here is that one methodology is not always going to be the best one. We should use Awareness and Whole Body Decisions™ to help us adapt our methodology to the particular needs of each project we are working on.

Take another look at the chameleon icon. There is a circle in the middle. The circle represents our core. Each of us has a set of ethics. We also have personal integrity and values. This core is non-negotiable. Whereas any given project management methodology should not be used in all situations, a value system absolutely should be applied in all situations. Further, experienced project managers are likely to have aspects of their project management approach that are part of their core. There may be certain tools or actions that you know will work every time you use them.

The Adaptability Discipline is about knowing when to adapt and when to use your core. This is not always an easy decision to make. If you are having difficulty deciding if you should adapt or not, go back to chapter six on Whole Body Decisions.™ It will provide you a framework to figure it out.

To Standardize or Not to Standardize

Conventional wisdom in the project management community calls for a standard approach to project management. A standard approach, the argument goes, provides consistency and interchangeability. With a standard approach, project managers can learn one way to do things instead of reinventing the wheel with every new project. Managers and executives will receive standardized reports that communicate what is happening across all projects. A standardized template for these reports will improve readability and understandability. The rest of the organization benefits as well, advocates of a standard approach argue. The rest of the organization knows what to expect from the project team. Also, it is argued, a standard approach will lead to projects that are more effective. In other words, they deliver the desired results as well as projects that are more efficient. They deliver those results with fewer resources and/or in a shorter period of time.

In this chapter, I showed the importance of adapting. I believe one of the legitimate questions this raises is, "How do I reconcile the Adaptability Discipline with the industry's call for a standard approach?"

The answer is to be smart about how you do both (create standards and adapt). When you create a standard approach, make sure that it leaves some room for adaptation. You can have a full-fledged project management methodology and a "methodology light" version that can be used on smaller projects. Another approach is to standardize certain aspects of the project environment, but not all aspects. For example, a standard report for an executive is very helpful. This report enables the project experts to communicate a broad array of information from multiple projects in a way that is clear and understandable. However, add an open-ended section of the report that allows for information to be communicated that does not fit neatly into the standard.

Adaptability, as mentioned, occurs within certain parameters. We do not want to adapt to everything that happens. A project manager who is constantly changing his or her mind is not likely to be viewed as a leader, and, worse, may be considered a "flip-flopper." However, some issues, which are considered part of the core, are not negotiable. A standard approach can be a great way to help assign this core.

Adaptability Exercises

Exercises to improve your Adaptability:

- "React to pushback" exercise. Think about one of the things that you are pushing in the project environment that's controversial. Using the process for Whole Body Decisions™, ask yourself, "Do I really need to keep pushing this particular report, idea, or process?" If the answer is no, then tell your team, "I thought about it. I listened to your feedback. I decided that we do not need to do this report anymore." They will respect you for it. Likewise, if you go through this exercise and determine that the item you are pushing is part of your core, then tell the team that you considered their input. You listened to them and you believe that the idea you are championing is still an important concept for the project team. Explain why you believe that. They will respect you for this decision as well. What's most important to the team is that you pay attention to the members. Demonstrate that you are evaluating their input and willing to adapt if necessary, but also willing to stick to your game plan when that's required.

- Methodology review. Take a look at your project management methodology from a fresh perspective. Take a step back and ask if it is achieving the goals you desire. Is it providing too much structure? Is it not providing enough structure? Develop a list of action items you and the project leadership at your organization can take to adapt the framework to what is best for your organization. Don't view this as a one-time-only event. Come back to this exercise regularly to reevaluate and tweak the methodology.

- "Question your assumptions" exercise. Pick something that you believe is true. Visualize it in your mind. Think about all of the aspects of this particular thought or idea that you think are true. Now, ask yourself, just for fun, to think about the world if it were not true. How would people act? What would be different? What if the exact opposite were true? Is there any reason to adapt your opinion? This is a good exercise to test our assumptions.

DIPLOMACY

The director of advertising and his manager sit opposite me and stare with looks of disappointment, anger, and disbelief. I have just told them that the financial plan our consulting team developed calls for a dramatic reduction in the total advertising spend. I have facts and figures to back up the reduction. However, I'm not sure anything in our analysis is going to change their minds, so I don't dwell on it.

We are sitting in the director's office. He has worked his way up to this position. He now has a very large advertising budget and the responsibility that comes along with it. He works for one of the world's largest automobile manufacturers. Neither one of us is sure what to say. There is an uncomfortable pause. I remind myself to stay calm and aware. It appears he is working hard to do the same. We both know we have a job to do. I need to get his support for the new budget. He needs to show top management that he is willing to be a part of the solution. He also needs to sell vehicles. The company is in trouble. Budgets need to be slashed. In some unique way, our interests are aligned. We both need to show progress.

I look him in the eye and tell him, as honestly and directly as possible, the reasons for the new budget. He replies with a seemingly honest assessment of where he thinks the budget number should be. We are having a conversation and that is what matters. At the end of the meeting, we have agreed to a few next steps that will keep the discussion moving forward. We have made headway, and, despite the difficult circumstances, built trust with each other.

This fairly simple approach of controlling yourself, being direct, keeping lines of communication open, and finding the slim space where your interests are aligned is a formula for diplomacy. I will come back to this shortly. First, let's talk about how people are wired. This will provide an important primer for diplomacy.

Brain Primer

Have you ever had conflict in one of your projects? I am guessing you have. Conflict is a consistent part of the landscape in a change management project. Part of the physiology of how we are wired as humans is that change creates stress. Projects can lead to the full range of human emotions, from encouragement to discouragement, from happiness to anger, and from laughter to tears.

This is why we need to understand diplomacy. Diplomacy, according to the *Encarta* dictionary, is "skill and tact in dealing with other people." In order to understand how to do this, we first need to understand how people are wired. Specifically, let's look into the brain.

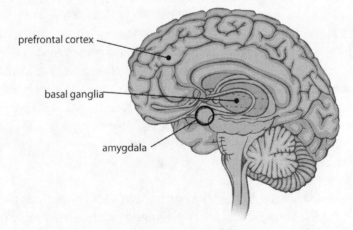

Exhibit 8-1 The Brain

Our prefrontal cortex includes working memory. Working memory is in the front of your brain, behind your forehead. Our working memory is where many scientists believe we process new and complex ideas. Using our working memory requires a lot of physical energy.

The basal ganglia are at the base of our brain. Often referred to as the reptilian mind, this is the oldest part of our brain. Our basal ganglia houses ideas and actions that we consider to be true. (Note: they may not actually be true, but we have convinced ourselves that they are and do not question their truth). Our basil ganglia do not require as much energy to operate as working memory.

Let's deepen our knowledge of these two parts of the brain by considering the example of driving a car. If you have been driving a car for twenty years then car driving is likely to be in your basal ganglia. In this case, you require less physical energy to drive than someone who is new to driving because the basal ganglia require less energy. However, if you are a teenager who has been driving a car for a grand total of twenty-three minutes, then car driving is likely to be a working memory exercise for you. It is going to take a lot more energy. New activities are typically working memory activities. Experienced drivers can sit in a car and drive for eight hours straight. They may be tired at the end of the journey, but a long drive is certainly possible. Can you imagine spending eight consecutive hours in the car training a teenager? Working memory activities are best performed in shorter periods of time with bursts of energy.

If working memory sends information to the basal ganglia that does not agree, it can cause an "error" message in the brain. An error message is the brain's way of telling us that something is not adding up. It is a warning. If the idea blends with what is in our basal ganglia then we can easily accept it and move on to the next issue. If it does not blend, we must either discard it or stop and think about it. In worst-case scenarios, the new error message can cause such turmoil in our brains that it can send us into the fight or flight response. In the fight response, we become more aggressive and begin to "attack" the person who presents this new idea. We challenge the idea. We might dispose of the idea outright. In the flight option, we disengage and remove ourselves from the situation.

With this brain primer as a baseline, now let's go back to the story at the beginning of the chapter. You will recall the four keys to diplomacy are controlling yourself, being direct, keeping lines of communication open, and finding the slim space where your interests are aligned.

Controlling Yourself

Diplomacy calls for us to remain in control. The emotions generated by a project environment can make it very difficult to stay in control. Consider the findings Daniel Goleman discusses in *Emotional Intelligence*. Mr. Goleman explains how our emotions can overtake our mental circuitry. The amygdala is the part of our brain that associates emotions with actions. A car flies past us on the shoulder of the highway. That's the action. Our amygdala tells us to get angry. That's the emotion. Someone delivers us flowers to the office. That's the action. Our amygdala tells us to be happy from this. That's the emotion.

When our emotions overtake us, the amygdala takes charge. This type of amygdala hijack occurs when something happens that causes us to be so emotional that it becomes difficult or impossible for us to think about anything other than the action causing the emotion. For example, we might get very angry when someone suddenly terminates our project. Our amygdala tells us to associate anger with the action of project cancellation. In an amygdala hijack, we are so consumed in that anger that we allow it to overtake us. In amygdala hijack, there is reduced blood flow to your frontal cortex, the thinking part of your brain. Literally, you are less able to reason through options and potential outcomes.

Further, our brains are wired in such a way that the message from our amygdala reaches us before our rational thought processes catch up. This is very useful when we need to instantaneously take actions to protect ourselves. Quickly after the amygdala sends the emotional response, unless we are in a full hijack, our rational brains will catch up and provide a more reasoned response.

What if you feel yourself going into an amygdala hijack? Unless you really need to run or fight, this is not going to be a good physical state for you because less blood will be flowing to the thinking part of your brain. You use this part of your brain to compare options and consequences. Further, the decreased use of working memory does not happen only in the extreme case of an amygdala hijack. Working memory can also be less capable as a result of less intense emotions.

If you are in a project situation, you are going to want to keep the thinking part of your brain active. You want to be able to think through options and outcomes. Here are three tricks you can deploy if you feel your emotions beginning to take over:

Take a Few Deep Breaths

Taking a few deep breaths is like a "reset" for your body. The five or ten seconds it takes you to breathe deeply might be just enough time to regain your composure. Those seconds can be enough to completely alter the way your brain processes what is happening. This brief moment, unless you are in a full amygdala hijack, may afford your rational brain time to catch up with the emotional impulse from the amygdala.

Take a Break

If you feel yourself getting into this state, it is usually a sign that you should back off. Call for a break in the meeting. Do something that gives you time to relax. Remember, an amygdala hijack means your emotions are in control of your actions. You have lost much, if not all, of your ability to reason through possible actions and outcomes. This is not a good state of mind to be in while leading a project or any other time.

Explain to Yourself Why the Action Might Be Okay

A third technique you can deploy is to develop a reasonable explanation for the exact behavior that is infuriating you. For example, let's say you are stuck in traffic on the freeway. All you can see in your windshield is red brake lights from what seems like a never-ending stream of cars in front of you. You look at your watch. You're going to be late again. Your stress level rises. Just at that point, a car goes speeding past you on the left shoulder. *Someone is cutting the line,* you tell yourself, *what a jerk!* At this point, you feel yourself going into fight or flight. You are angry and you're looking for an outlet to unleash that anger. Here's what you can do: think of an explanation for that car's behavior that would make it acceptable. Say to yourself something like this: *Maybe the driver of that car just found out his father is in the hospital. The driver must be in a rush to get there. I am glad that the shoulder was open so he could get there quickly.* Or you might say to yourself, *I noticed there was a woman leaning back in the passenger seat. Perhaps she is in labor. It is fortunate that the shoulder lane was open so she can get to the hospital to have her baby.* Thinking about these more acceptable behaviors may diffuse your anger.

You are intelligent enough to know the difference between the truth and the mental trick that you just deployed to calm yourself down. The reason why you are doing this is to keep yourself under control. By telling yourself these stories, you have enabled blood to start flowing back to the thinking part of your brain. You have regained control over your body, your decisions, and your actions.

On a personal note, a year or so ago I was a passenger in a car that was stopped at a traffic light. The driver of the car behind us was furiously honking her car's horn and flashing lights. We looked at the car, trying to figure out what was going on. At that moment, a desperate woman jumped out of the driver's side leaving the door open. She ran up to our car and tapped on the driver's window. "My dog is dying!" she yelled, obviously in grief. "I need to make a right turn to get to the veterinarian right now. Can you let me through?" She pointed to our car blocking her path. We moved our car and let her pass. Sometimes there *really is* a good explanation for why people act the way they do.

Help Other People Stay in Control Too

Of course, you can't control other people. However, you can take some actions that will help them remain calm. Let's reconsider the brain primer. For many people in your project, the change is going to be a working memory type of activity. That means it will require more energy for his or her brain to process the change. It also means that they will not be able to sustain a high level of activity for a long period of time. This may have important implications for your team meetings. Schedule your initial team meetings for a shorter period, not more than four to six hours of heavy work. Give people time to process what is going on. After people become familiar with the concepts, you can transition into longer meetings.

Your awareness will tell you when to call it quits. When people are in the middle of heavy working memory processing, they may have a "deer in the headlights" appearance—that is, a gaze off into the distance or a relatively expressionless face. They may not say much or move much. They are processing. When you see that look in your team member's faces, it may be time to end the meeting. Whatever you say now is not going to be processed. Give them a break and come back tomorrow.

You can also help other people stay in control by mapping the change to something familiar. Research shows that one of the best ways to help people process new changes is to map what is new to what is familiar. If I tell you about a brand new gadget I am inventing, then you are forced to create an entirely new space in your mind for this concept. Many people find this difficult. On the other hand, if I tell you that this gadget is like a Slinky, except longer and wider, then you have a visual image. You are much closer to understanding what I'm talking about. Analogies are a great way to map what is new to what is familiar.

Decisions, of course, do not always lead to extreme emotions. However, there typically is some level of emotion corresponding to a decision. This is okay and natural. It is important to identify when it occurs. When you see people becoming emotional, even a little bit, it is best to give them time to process things. New research shows that even lower-grade emotions can activate the amygdala and simultaneously decrease the capabilities of our working memory, the thinking part of our brain. People need to work through decisions in their own way. Give them space and time to do that.

Be Direct

Build a reputation as a person who is true to his or her word. When you are in diplomatic situations that call for you to work through conflict or disagreement, your word will become invaluable. Honestly and openly tell people the situation as you know it. Ask them to do the same. Direct, frank conversation provides a solid starting point for a diplomatic discussion.

Be Direct about Your Needs

At face value, it may appear that you and the other party are on opposite sides of the coin. If you focus discussions on your position versus their position, then you are going to have a more difficult time reaching agreement. In some cases, a me-versus-you discussion makes your challenge even more difficult by pushing the other party further into their opinion. If, however, you focus on needs, then you may be able to develop a creative way to keep everyone happy. Tell the person the needs that are underlying your recommendation. In the case of the story above, my need was to make the numbers work in the financial forecast. The director of advertising needed to have an effective advertising campaign. That's the starting point. Contrast this to a position-based approach where I might have taken the position that the budget needed to be one number and the director took a position that the budget must be a different number. Taking positions like this can create winners and losers and make for a much more difficult negotiation.

Be Direct about the Scope of the Team

Help team members understand the scope of their role. For example, let's say the project team is designing a new organization. The team is populated with middle-level managers with a lot of experience and knowledge about the organization's inner workings. This group will be a great resource for designing new processes and procedures. However, they may not be the best resource to design the organizational structure and compensation plan for the new group. You may need to turn to subject matter experts and an executive steering group for this type of design. Whatever you choose, be upfront with the team and let them know from day one they will be, in this case, designing processes and procedures but not an organizational chart and a compensation program.

Be Direct about Expectations

People are better able to handle major changes if they know what to expect. Consider the following story. Years ago, I earned an instrument rating to add to my private pilot's license. To earn an instrument rating, you must learn how to fly the aircraft solely with reference to the instruments in the cockpit. You are not permitted to look outside for visual cues. While paying attention to the instruments, you are also operating the radios and navigating the airplane. I had previously earned a private pilot's license. Also, I already had some experience flying the airplane on instruments. Nonetheless, my flight instructor told me I would hit a wall in the middle of my training. He said everyone did. Further, he said I was likely to regress. In order to fly the plane on instruments while operating radios and navigating, you must rethink how you do things.

Sure enough, midway through my instrument training I hit the wall. When that happened, I knew that I was not alone. Everyone else hits the wall too, I told myself. Even though my piloting abilities temporarily became worse, I had confidence it would improve to an even higher level after I learned how to retool what I had previously learned into a more holistic approach to the airplane. I made it through to completion because my flight instructor had managed my expectations.

Years later, I was the director of a flight school in the Chicagoland area. A middle-aged student walked into my office. He was a successful professional who was not accustomed to failing. However, that day he was clearly agitated. He was in the middle of instrument training and he had hit that wall.

"I can't do it," he told me. "I'm too old."

I explained to him that everyone went through this. I said, "Didn't your instructor tell you that at the beginning of your training?"

"No," he said.

I was not able to convince him that his experience was customary. He left and did not return. Contrast this to my flying experience where I was prepared for initial failure because I was told to expect difficulty. When it occurred to me, I was ready for it because someone had managed my expectations. However, this gentleman's expectations were not managed. He expected to keep on flying successfully like he always had. He was not too old. He just hit the wall that everyone hits. I could not convince him at that moment that everyone else went through a similar experience. It did not sound credible. If someone had told him earlier, he would have been more likely to believe the message. Now, it just sounded like I was trying to make him feel better.

Let's apply this to the project environment. We are leading change. There are going to be rough spots. I believe our best approach is to let people know that. Manage their expectations. Do not lead them to believe project managers have some magic wand that makes everything smooth and easy. We do not. What we can do is navigate those treacherous waters to deliver results. But there will still be treacherous waters.

When I tell people that I focus on the human side of change, sometimes they say, "So you have figured out a way to manage change without conflict. You make it easy, right?" No. I have figured out a way to deliver results. There is a big difference. A Sixth Sense for Project Management® is about delivering results. However, sometimes the way we do that is not easy.

Keep Lines of Communication Open

Diplomacy is about dialogue. Do whatever you can to keep the conversation going. If you are talking, there is still a chance, no matter how slim, that you may be able to work it out. When conversation ends, the challenge becomes much taller.

One of the keys to diplomatic communication is to communicate in a way that is collaborative, consistent, and authentic. *Harvard Business*

Review published an article titled "Why It's So Hard to Be Fair" authored by Joel Brockner. This article argues that people are more likely to pay attention to the process one uses rather than the outcome. This is so important that it bears repeating for emphasis. *According to research, people are more concerned about how they are treated and the perceived fairness of a process than the outcome of that process.* Consider the following studies:

Example #1 - Wrongful Termination Lawsuits
Research conducted by Allan Lind and Jerald Greenberg found that 1 percent of ex-employees who felt that they were treated with a very fair process filed a wrongful termination lawsuit; whereas 15 percent of those who believe they were treated with a very unfair process filed suit.

Example #2 – Medical Malpractice Lawsuits
Surprisingly, physicians who deliver poor quality care for their patients do not get sued more than those who provide higher quality care. Researcher Wendy Levinson found, however, that the quality of interpersonal skills does make a difference. Primary care physicians are less likely to be sued if they educate patients about what to expect, use more humor, ask patients' opinions, confirm understanding, and ask them to talk. Good bedside manner makes a real difference.

Both of these examples show that *how* professionals perform their work is considered to be more important than the outcome of the work. I do not mean to say that results are unimportant. As mentioned in chapter one, Roeder Consulting is absolutely focused on delivering results. Our 90 percent success rate demonstrates our commitment to results. However, research, such as the studies mentioned above, shows us that the ends typically do not justify the means when it comes to change. Said differently, the path you take to deliver results matters … *a lot.*

Recently, a high-profile example brought this concept to light. LeBron James, a well-known player in the National Basketball Association, decided to leave the Cleveland Cavaliers and sign with the Miami Heat. Some people liked this decision and some people did not. There is a mixed verdict on the outcome. However, what many people did not like is *how* the decision was announced. Mr. James went on live national television to announce that he had decided to go to the Heat. Many considered this an inappropriate way to make this announcement. They would have preferred an announcement that was not broadcast on live television and more discrete.

Many people did not think the process was fair. Their perception was that the way the decision was communicated was not appropriate. It is important for us to understand this human dynamic in our projects. Your project will be judged not only by the outcome, but also by the methods you use to achieve and communicate that outcome.

In chapter six, which included the Clear Communication Discipline, I described ways to accurately share information. Building on this, I will now discuss how to communicate in a way that is diplomatic. That is, how to communicate in a way that is more likely to garner good will, relationship-building, and support for your project. Following the three steps below will help you avoid situations like those described above.

Collaborative Communication

Few things get people more upset than having a change forced on them. People might say, "If only the project manager had asked me, I could have explained ..." Actively soliciting input not only helps people feel like they are part of the process, but it also helps you get a better answer overall. If you solicit input, it is critical that you know what to do with the information once you receive it. Asking people for their opinions, and then promptly discarding or ignoring their input, will backfire. If you are going to ask for input, you need to be prepared to either incorporate it into your project or have a very good answer as to why the input was not part of the final recommendation.

Authentic Communication

It is self-evident that people desire to be treated with respect. More specifically, people want others to actively listen to them and show real concern. People expect you to pay attention to what they are saying and to respond with well thought-out and complete answers. An answer that is flippant is worse than no answer at all. The concern a person shares may not be important to you, but it is sure important to him or her. If you want to treat the person with respect, take his or her concern to heart. Communication that is not perceived to be authentic is worse than no communication at all. (See LeBron James.)

Consistent Approach and Communication

Some individuals who are on the receiving end of a change project seem to have highly tuned radar for even the slightest inconsistencies. Some people walk around like a roaming "consistency meter." Even the slightest inconsistency in your approach or communications and they will signal the flashing lights and alarm bells. In their defense, these people are often motivated by a desire for fairness. It is important to them, and to us too, that everyone in the organization is treated in a fair and consistent manner throughout the change process. Diplomatically addressing these people, as well as the rest of your organization, means having a consistent and fair approach to how key decisions are made and communicated.

Find Common Ground

Seek areas where you can agree with the other party. Even if it is something very small, starting dialogue with an agreement can provide momentum to the process and confidence that the logjam can be worked through. This takes real creativity at times. Keep your mind open and find that narrow sliver where you can agree.

As the conversation progresses, determine ways to continuously find common ground. However, don't be surprised if there is still conflict. Conflict and emotions come along with change.

Be Patient When Seeking Common Ground

People need time to process change. This is tricky for many project managers. We have work plans. We have deadlines. We need people to move now. The truth about how we are wired as human beings is that we don't change our behaviors based on someone else's timeline. We change our behaviors, if at all, on our own timeline. I will discuss this in more detail in the following chapter. Part of A Sixth Sense for Project Management® is knowing how to reconcile the time constraints of your project with the physiological constraints of those who are changing.

Also, consider the effects of emotions and anger on projects. Have you ever seen someone cry in the project environment? Have you seen people get angry? Have people been very excited? Emotions come along for the ride. Let's consider the case of anger. When we become upset, certain "angry chemicals" are released into our bloodstream. These "angry chemicals" can take anywhere from several hours to several days to flush out of our bloodstream. The whole time these "angry chemicals" are in our bloodstream, we are more likely to be edgy. Add to these chemicals the neurological response of an amygdala hijack and very quickly you have an irate and irrational person on your hands.

Also, consider that the time required to flush out these angry chemicals is dependent on what else is going on. A fast flushing of them might mean sitting on your favorite beach with a cocktail in your hand. In our regular daily lives, we often go from one meeting to another. More stress is created. We drive home and the car gets a flat tire. More stress. We arrive home and learn that a pipe burst in our basement. More stress. Evidence shows, in some cases, that an extreme event can permanently change how we are wired. Some people who experience deep trauma may truly never be the same again. The bottom line is that we must learn how to recognize these responses to change and deploy the tools discussed in this chapter to mitigate them.

Diplomacy Exercises

Exercises to improve your Diplomacy:

- The "create a third option" exercise. This exercise is a combination of the Adaptability and Diplomacy Disciplines. Identify a sticking point in one of your projects. Pick a situation where you just can't do it the way one of the key stakeholders has asked for, and he or she can't accept your way. Think about a third way to resolve the dispute. Get creative. It might be a "halfway" solution that is somewhere between your two perspectives. Or it could be something completely different. Instead of devoting a lot of your energy arguing your idea versus theirs, try to find a solution that is agreeable to all. Note: there will be some times when you need to fight the good fight if the attribute is a "must have" for your project. This exercise refers to everything else.

- Manage expectations. Think about something that you know will be occurring soon on one of your projects. Ask yourself if the team knows about this upcoming event. Do the stakeholders know? If they don't, let them know. This is a good exercise to remind us that other people may not know what we do. Informing them will help the feel more connected to the process.

- Get into someone else's "odds are." When I was in sales, I was taught that the "odds are" that people are thinking about themselves and not about you. Think about a person in your project. Put yourself in his or her shoes. How is the project impacting her? What would make the project more successful from her standpoint? How might her perspective change over time? By putting yourself in her shoes, you'll better understand her reasoning. This exercise helps us see our project from different viewpoints. The ability to see the project from multiple viewpoints is a great start toward being more diplomatic.

PERSISTENCE

A married couple, we'll call them Jack and Diane, sit in their living room watching a cooking show. Their apartment is small but adequate. They share a happy gaze with each other. At that moment, an advertisement appears on the television. The advertisement is for a red sports car with a turbo-charged engine. *Boy,* Jack thinks, *does that look like fun.*

"Wouldn't it be great to get that car?" Jack says to Diane.

"What?" Diane asks.

"That car, the one in this television commercial," he says as he points to the screen. "Wouldn't it be nice to have one of those?"

"Are you crazy?" Diane says. "There is no way you are going to get that car. Do you remember the last new car we purchased? You crashed it into the telephone pole next to our driveway. And how are we going to pay for it?" Jack goes to the floor and pleads. Diane says, "What are you doing? Get off your knees."

Jack returns to his chair from the position he had taken in front of his wife to beg for the sports car. Now he wants that car more than ever. For some reason, being told "No" by his wife has made the desire even greater. He had crashed the prior car. That was true. He also knew they could not afford the car. But the facts did not change his desire. No matter how many facts Diane could throw at him, something in his body yearned for that car.

I use this fictional story to highlight two important truths about people. First, when we take an emotional position, we are not likely to be persuaded by the facts. Second, once we stake out a position, we are likely to dig in our heels even more deeply when someone challenges our opinion, even if it was a loosely held opinion to begin with. I'll come back to this later in the chapter and tie it into the Persistence Discipline. First, let's define persistence.

Find the Path to Success with Persistence

Projects rarely flow in a straight line. We need to figure out how to go over, under, or through our challenges to be successful. In our discussions and surveys of project managers, persistence frequently comes up as a key to success. Many project managers, particularly more experienced ones, count persistence as a key factor in their success. This chapter will focus on what I call "patient persistence." First, let's look at the word "persistence."

Persistence, according to *Webster's Dictionary*, has three definitions: continuing, especially in the face of opposition; continuing to exist or endure; constantly repeated. Each of these three definitions has a place in project management.

Continuing, Especially in the Face of Opposition

In the chapter on adaptability, I demonstrated that tension and emotions accompany times of change. This creates a difficult environment. At times, a challenging project environment can make it difficult to get up in the morning and resume work on the project. Successful project managers possess a tenacity that keeps them going. They just "keep on keepin' on" until they get the results they need.

Many times this is done in the face of opposition. What makes it even trickier is that you are never quite sure where that opposition is going to come from. There are the usual suspects. For example, the stakeholder who does not appreciate your project because it is rendering outdated something he implemented in prior years. Another example is an executive who is concerned about the political ramifications of the project. This type of resistance is not unusual. However, sometimes we also get resistance from within our ranks. A team member may resist us for unexpected, and often unknown, reasons. Someone superior to us in the project management structure might start asking us unfamiliar and unexpected questions. Whatever the case might be in your situation, it is fair to say that many project managers regularly operate in the face of opposition. Blasting through this requires steely persistence.

Continuing to Exist or Endure

These are not the most cheery words. "Continuing to exist" makes it sound like persistence is more about hanging on than proactively driving change. I suppose, in some cases this is an accurate statement. All of us can probably remember days when we just tried to hang on. Sometimes, we just need to do our best to keep going until the clouds clear. How about the word "endure"? I'll leave it to you to make the final judgment here. Are there some moments in project management that you just have to endure?

Constantly Repeated

Many people associate persistence with coming back over and over again until you get the desired result. This type of persistence is part of successful project management. Sometimes, people need to be hounded to get things done. This might not be enjoyable for us, but it is necessary. People often need to be reminded to get their reports in. Others will not complete their deliverables unless the project manager is present, whip in hand, making it happen.

Keeping people on task is more important than ever. Organizations are becoming more efficient and that means fewer people are employed to do the work. There are more projects under way. People are increasingly spread thin. This means some people simply go from one fire to the next. In this environment, the project manager needs to stand tall and work diligently to keep team members actively engaged.

We must be persistent on our efforts to ensure people follow through. However, we still want to be diplomatic and sensitive to others. Being persistent does not mean being annoying. When you ask for reports, do it with a smile on your face. When you remind people about their deliverable, tell them that you understand they are very busy. Work with people to figure out creative ways to get the deliverable done within the context of their abilities and availability. This empathy will help soothe people and build their trust in you. Be a project leader, not a taskmaster.

Patient Persistence

Persistence must be used with caution. There is a line between pushing hard to deliver project results and being too aggressive in a way that pushes people away from you. I use the term "patient persistence" to describe what this discipline is really about. With patient persistence, we certainly remain true to our project goal. We lay out a path that provides ample time not only for the tasks to be completed, but also for the people who must change to have proper time to go through the emotional process required. This may take considerable patience.

Forcing the Facts on People May Backfire

One area where patient persistence is needed is when there is significant disagreement. Research indicates that once people establish an opinion, they tend to embrace additional information only when it supports their current view. People tend to want to think they are right. They like evidence that tells them they are right. When they are presented with facts that indicate otherwise, they may resist this new information. Interestingly, in some cases the new, accurate information may backfire and actually push people even deeper into their current misguided opinion. Many opinions are formed more by belief than by facts.

Pushing Stakeholders for Answers May Lead to Undesirable Results

Project managers, I have established, typically must get things done through other people. We need other people to approve our scope. We need other people to sign off on the budget. Sometimes stakeholders do not readily have answers for us. So we push them harder to provide those answers. This may be counterproductive.

Projects will be more successful if we capture what is known upfront but avoid forcing people to falsely provide clarity that is not there yet. Said differently, do not force stakeholders for answers to questions that are currently unanswerable. For example, as project managers, we know that it is important to be comprehensive when gathering requirements. As specifically as possible, we want details from our stakeholders on everything related to the project, from budget to resources to timelines. Sometimes, this causes us to force our stakeholders into premature positions on the project. They may not have full clarity on the project yet. Things might be shifting and evolving. The executive stakeholder may have a business need that should be filled, but has not completely clarified how to fill it or how it fits the project into other pieces of the businesses. In the middle of the confusion, the project manager comes along saying, "Just define everything for me so I can make it happen." What we may be doing in these circumstances is prematurely forcing that stakeholder into a position.

When we force someone into an opinion, he or she is probably going to defend it later on, even if it is loosely held and even if it was made in error, perhaps too prematurely. Through a patient kind of persistence, there is a better way. A Sixth Sense for Project Management® tells us people are going to be better off if we capture what is known upfront, but avoid forcing people to falsely provide clarity that is not there yet.

Our Profession Is Adapting by Creating More Flexible Approaches.

This phenomenon of forcing people into premature positions in project management has been part of the catalyst for more flexible approaches to project management, such as Agile. In February, 2001, seventeen people met at a ski resort in Utah and created the Agile Software Development Manifesto. Since then, agile project management has grown rapidly. The PMBOK® Guide currently advocates a more linear waterfall method where projects are initiated, then planned, then executed and controlled, and so on. The Agile approach puts much less emphasis on a linear planning approach and more emphasis on setting a vision, and then using shorter-cycle efforts to deliver results. Planning happens on an ongoing basis.

One of the principles of the manifesto is to "Welcome changing requirements, even late in development …" Welcoming changing requirements late in the project was certainly not a principle I was taught when I received my Project Management Professional certification years ago. This is a welcome change.

Give People Time

If you have a heated team meeting that elevates someone else's angry chemicals, you are confronting, chemically, a different person than you might experience just a few hours later. When you are pushing hard, ask yourself if you need to push that hard right now. The unpleasant reality is that the way we are wired as people does not always fit well with our project timeline. Negotiating this disconnect requires adaptability and persistence.

So when we talk about persistence we need to be careful not to overdo it. Keep persistent to your project goals and deliverables. Keep persistent to expecting people to deliver what they have committed. However, when you are doing the hard work to change beliefs and behaviors, you will need patient persistence.

Let's go back to the story that opened this chapter. Jack wants a new car. Diane confronts Jack with several facts, including that they can't afford the car and Jack crashed the last car. However, Jack does not change his mind. Even thought Diane is correct, these truths are not going to make him change his mind. His desire is based on an emotional need that does not go away simply because new facts emerge. Further, the harder she pushes him, the more likely he is to want the car even more. Her pushing is counterproductive.

This dynamic happens in projects all the time. Project leadership pushes for a new way to do things by advancing business cases, facts, and figures. Others in the organization have an emotional response to the change. The facts and figures don't change their emotions so they continue to resist the change. Project leadership pushes the facts even harder and the resistance becomes fiercer. This spiral of increasing discontent can be mitigated by deploying patient persistence. Give people time to embrace the change on their own terms. Help them along the emotional journey of change.

Enduring Change

Finally, in the category of persistence, I also include implementing changes that are enduring. People may behave differently during project implementation versus afterward. Studies show that people change their behavior when they know they are being watched. In the well-known Hawthorne Study, factory workers were told that their productivity was going to be observed. With no further actions, the performance of the factory workers improved. In other words, simply being told that someone was watching was enough for them to regulate their own behavior and adjust. The people who were told they were being observed adjusted their behavior in a way they felt was desired by those watching.

This phenomenon occurs in our projects too. Projects often bring a large spotlight of energy and attention to a certain area of the organization. When people are standing in the middle of the spotlight, they may do what they think is desired. However, as soon as the project spotlight moves away, people often return to their previous behavior … or to some other set of undesirable behaviors. Fortunately, there are actions we can take to make our changes sustainable after the spotlight of the project goes away. Those steps follow.

Specific

People must know, as specifically as possible, what actions and behaviors are desired. Many projects implement with people unsure about what it means to them. "Okay, so we have a new system," they might say. "Now what?" Successful leaders of enduring change provide very specific directions to those who are impacted by the change. At the end of this section on hardwiring change, you will see a list of items you can put in place to make change enduring. Note how each of them can be made to be very specific.

Written

Putting desired behaviors in writing achieves several goals. First, it reinforces the verbal project announcements and presentations. Second, written materials are enduring. If the current people transition out of their roles, written guidance will inform the new people what to do. Written directions are critical to enduring change.

Mandatory

If you truly desire to change behavior, then the new behaviors must be required. Long ago, it was decided that a change was needed regarding how cars travel on the roads in the United States. Stop signs were put in place. None of them are optional. If they were, they would not have any value.

Do not offer wiggle room where people can revert to the old way of doing things. I have seen people take the easy route in the final moments of change and make the changes optional. In the final moments, when the new way is ever so close to being the law of the land, sometimes the battles are fiercest. Do not allow the new way to be optional. If it is truly a better way to do things, then why not require everyone to do it that way? You may negotiate a delayed implementation, but the new way must still be required once implemented.

Designated Enforcer

A specific role in your organization must be assigned the responsibility of enforcing the new order. If possible, write it into the job description. Without identifying a single role, you risk having no one in charge. Have you heard the saying, "When everyone is in charge, no one is in charge"? This is the case with post-implementation changes. Put someone in charge. Also, be sure to designate a role (as in a job title) and not a person. People may come and go but the roles they are in will stay in place until they are consciously changed.

When you put these four together—specific, written, mandatory, and assigning a designated enforcer—you will be well on your way toward persistent, enduring change. Here are a few examples of items that, if structured correctly, provide this type of enduring change:

- Processes
- Roles and responsibilities
- Job descriptions
- Organizational structure
- Incentives (compensation, rewards, and recognition)
- Performance management
- Metrics

One final note: do not wait until the end of the project to put these tools in place. From the very early days you should think about ways to integrate sustainable techniques into the project management process. For example, if you need people to do something differently when the project implements, then ask for their job descriptions to be placed into the project scope. If you are designing a new process, then mobilize the resources required to document that process and integrate it into the organization's doctrine.

Persistence Exercises

Exercises to improve your persistence:

- The "back off" exercise. Identify a situation where you are aggressively pushing for change. Ask yourself if you need to push so hard. Can you give people extra time to process the change? Can you deploy the slow, patient kind of persistence? If you can, make the change. This exercise helps us differentiate what is truly urgent from everything else.

- "Test the wiring" exercise. Ask yourself if you have taken appropriate steps to hardwire the changes your project is pursuing. Have you put items in place that are specific, written, mandatory, and enforced by a specific role in the organization? If the answer is "No," then figure out ways you can start doing this today. This exercise helps you ensure your changes stay in place after you move on to the next project. This will help build your legacy not only for successfully driving changes, but also for creating the infrastructure for those changes to be sustainable for as long as is necessary.

- "A new way" exercise. Persistence can be about breaking through obstacles in your path. Also, it can be about figuring out new ways to go over, under, and around those obstacles. Visualize the largest obstacle to success in your project. Now, think through ways you can get past the obstacle. Do you need to bust through it? If so, how will you accomplish that? Or can you get around the obstacle some other way? If so, how will that be done? This exercise opens our minds to possibilities. We keep obstacles under control by visualizing ways to manage them effectively.

SECTION THREE

THE JOURNEY

Section two covered the six disciplines that make up A Sixth Sense for Project Management®. Each of these disciplines represents a skill we can identify and improve. In section three, I shift our attention to the journey that one must take to truly understand these disciplines.

Proper application of the disciplines will lead to deeper intuition. In chapter ten I will explain intuition in detail. As you proceed along your personal journey toward improved interpersonal skills, you will also likely improve your intuition.

Finally, in chapter eleven I will discuss the intangible components of A Sixth Sense for Project Management®. In this thought-provoking and inspirational chapter, I also invite you to join us on the journey to an improved understanding of the human experience during times of change.

 **INTUITION**

When I discuss A Sixth Sense for Project Management,® many people's minds go directly to intuition. The words "sixth sense" and "intuition" connote something intangible and powerful. Indeed, there is a relationship between A Sixth Sense for Project Management® and intuition. Intuition cuts across several disciplines. Intuition is an expert application of Awareness, Whole Body Decisions,™ and Adaptability.

What Is Intuition?

"Intuition" is derived from the Latin word *intueri,* which means "to look inside" or "to contemplate." Consider the following facts about intuition:

- Psychologist Carl Jung identified intuition as one of four personality types in his 1921 book *Psychological Types.*

- During World War II, Katharine Cook Briggs and her daughter, Isabel Briggs Myers, were looking for a way to help women entering the workforce. They built a questionnaire based on Jung's research that would eventually become the "Myers Briggs Type Indicator." This is one of the most widely used personality profiles in the world. One of the main attributes it measures is intuition.

- Intuition can lead to faster decisions and improved quality of decisions, and it is a critical tool in a well-rounded "tool kit."

Intuition is a critical skill for professionals striving to be at the top of their field. Yet few people are formally trained on intuition. I will focus on what I have named "experienced intuition." Experienced intuition occurs when deep awareness and experience are synthesized into intuitive insights.

Experienced Intuition

Experienced intuition is frequently reported from people who have deep knowledge and experience in the area where they are receiving intuition. For example, a surgeon who finds unusual circumstances during a procedure may use her intuition to determine the best course of action. It may be difficult to determine if the surgeon's actions are guided by training, experience, or by some sort of intuition that synthesizes her collective knowledge and experiences into an action. Recently, I had dinner with a friend who is a hospice doctor. She explained many circumstances where she uses intuition to determine the best approach. She said it's difficult to say if her intuition is coming from her years of training in medical school, her decade or more of experience, or some other source. This melding of knowledge, education, and insight is a common characteristic of "experienced intuition."

Spontaneous Intuition

A second type of intuition is "spontaneous intuition." Spontaneous intuition occurs when people receive a vision, a message, or a feeling from undetermined sources. People might ask themselves, *Where did that come from?* Unlike experienced intuition, in spontaneous intuition it is not possible to trace the intuitive moment to formal education or one's professional experiences. For example, a person has a bad feeling about walking into the grocery store. She acts on this feeling and turns around before walking in the front door. Moments later there is a thunderous roar as a piece of equipment just inside the door comes crashing down. If she had entered the door, she surely would have been hit. This intuitive moment can't be traced to formal education or work-related experience. Something else is going on and that's a marker of "spontaneous intuition." More research is needed to understand spontaneous intuition. For the remainder of this chapter, I will focus on experienced intuition. Intuition is often best understood through examples. Therefore, I will start by looking at several examples to bring light to the dynamics of intuition.

Examples of Experienced Intuition

On January 15, 2009, US Airways flight #1549 successfully landed in the Hudson River after a dangerous midair collision with waterfowl. The Airbus A320 was piloted by Captain James Sullenberger, also known as "Sully," and First Officer Jeff Skiles. Both engines in the airplane were incapacitated by the bird strike. In an interview with Katie Couric from CBS News, Captain Sullenberger reported that just after seeing the birds he "felt, heard, and smelled the evidence" of the bird strike.

After conquering his initial reaction of disbelief, Sully went through a logical decision-making process: *Should I immediately turn around,* he reasoned, *to land at the same airport where I took off? No, that will take us over a densely populated area and put the lives of many on the ground at stake. Can I make it to another airport? No. Can I restart the engines? Maybe. I am going to give it a shot.*

Sully and the first officer executed engine restart procedures without success. By a process of elimination, Sully came to the grim conclusion that his best option was to land the plane in the Hudson River. The next action was certainly guided by intuition. He had never landed a commercial airliner in the water before. Simulators are not able to fully replicate the experience either. Captain Sullenberger knew that he needed to touch down with "the wings exactly level, the nose slightly up … and … just above our minimum flying speed but not below it."

Then, he did what many people thought was impossible. He landed a commercial airliner in the Hudson River and everyone survived. Sully called on a deep awareness of the situation and years of experience to make decisions and take unprecedented actions. Sully does not report having hunches other than saying, "I was sure I could do it." People experiencing intuition often report "knowing" that a certain outcome is correct or a certain action can be successfully completed.

Sully's story shows how years of training and deep experience can meld with deep awareness to create intuition. In the case of Flight #1549, intuition led to spectacular results. At the time of the incident, Captain Sullenberger had forty-two years of flight experience. However, this flight experience would not have mattered without his awareness. His awareness told him why the airplane experienced a loss of engine power. Also, his situational awareness told him where he was, how much time he had before touchdown, and other important pieces of information required for a successful outcome. This story highlights the important role awareness plays in intuition.

Next, consider the fascinating story of Argentinean race-car driver Juan Fangio. Mr. Fangio drove Formula One cars in the sport's early days. In 1950, he won the Monaco Grand Prix by famously avoiding an accident. The accident occurred in a turn that was ahead of him and out of sight. Even though he could not see the accident, Mr. Fangio slowed down. How did he know to do this? After the race and some thought, Mr. Fangio said his view of the fans told him there was trouble. He was the lead car. People, he reasoned, usually look at the lead car. With people looking at him he should see a lighter blur as he drove by. Instead, Mr. Fangio explained, he saw a darker blur indicating hair from heads that were turned. People were looking ahead of him, indicating there must be some kind of trouble. Mr. Fangio's intuition led him to victory.

Both of these situations depict seasoned professionals applying their deep knowledge and expertise in unconventional ways. Experienced intuition is a deep awareness coupled with experience to lead the conscious and unconscious mind to deliver exceptional insights. Our unconscious mind runs in the background processing information. Intuition, in part, comes from an ability to listen to these messages and decipher them. Deciphering is required because the unconscious mind often works in images and abstractions.

It is easy to imagine Mr. Fangio telling himself not to worry about a blur of fans. How often do we do this in our own lives? We get a feeling about something, but we tell ourselves the feeling is trivial or incorrect. People at the top of their field learn to listen to these gut feelings. They also become expert at telling when these feelings are correct.

Developing Your Intuition

Intuition is facilitated by stillness, awareness, experience, and training. You can develop or enhance your own intuition by working on each.

Stillness

The first step toward intuition is to do nothing. Literally, try not to do anything. Create quiet time for yourself. Relax in a comfortable setting. Close your eyes. Take a few deep breaths. Clear you mind. Stillness facilitates intuition. This does not mean intuition happens only during quiet times. You may be taking a shower or running to the store when an idea pops into your mind. Indeed, Mr. Fangio was at the helm of a lightning-fast car when his intuition struck. However, it is likely that he quieted the "noise" in his mind to create room for exactly the type of message he received. After you slow down and create quiet, tell yourself you are open to intuition. Your intuition does not have value if you don't listen to it.

Awareness

After you open space for intuition to occur, the next step is to pay attention. "Look within," as the Latin derivation of the word intuition tells us. How do you make decisions? How do different situations impact you physically and emotionally? Expand your awareness by asking the same questions of other people. How do they process the world around them? What changes their behaviors? What are the physical characteristics of your surroundings? What is happening in the larger context? Are you working in a group that has just been downsized? Is your organization struggling to keep up? See chapter four for a detailed discussion of awareness.

Experience

The more experience you have, the more likely you are to use intuition. So one way to improve your intuition is to be patient and let your career progress. However, there are "experience accelerators" that can help you develop intuition more quickly. One experience accelerator is to have a mentor. Good mentors share their experiences with us in a way that might make those experiences our own. They help us understand what is going on and why. Another experience accelerator is to put yourself in a position that stretches your abilities. Work on a larger project, a different type of project, an uncomfortable project. This push on your abilities will improve your intuition more rapidly.

Training

Perhaps the most powerful "experience accelerator" is professional and personal development. Attend sessions that challenge your thinking. Work on developing your skills related to the human side of change. In chapter one, I showed in detail the correlation between the project manager's people skills and project success. Also, professional development is a great way to meet other colleagues and hear how they succeed. Think of these people as "one-day mentors" who are accelerating your experience.

Intuition is a muscle that can be developed. By taking the actions above, you will strengthen this muscle. Initially, the muscle may be weak. Over time, it can become strong and powerful.

When Is Intuition Accurate?

Thoughts, visions, and ideas are not always accurate. We need a complex system of crosschecks to validate these thoughts. As discussed previously, Roeder Consulting calls this complex system Whole Body Decisions™, incorporating input from your brain, your heart, and your gut.

If your intuition tells you to take the project in a certain direction, check the data to see if it supports your intuition. Intuition works the other way around too. Spend a lot of time studying the data, and then let your subconscious mind sort it out while you go for a walk, sleep, or do something else unrelated to the work. You may experience moments of intuition after your full body has had time to process the data.

Many Project Managers Already Use Intuition

Intuition is a tool many project managers already use. Research shows that project managers often deploy intuition when there is too much data or not enough. Intuition may also be called upon when under a time crunch to make decisions. A project environment can often be fast-moving and dynamic. In this environment, sometimes the facts are antiquated or insufficient. Intuition can be the perfect tool to find the path to clarity.

Interestingly, many project managers deploy intuition covertly.

> "Knowledgeable and experienced project managers are tasked to deliver outcomes within organizations quickly and incurring the minimum of risk. However, moving away from a documented plan is seen as risky, and the safety net of joint planning and agreement on schemas of action is removed when a project manager decides to improvise … In Agor's study of intuition nearly half the respondents indicated that they kept the fact that they relied upon intuition a secret, whilst others reported a post-hoc rationalization for decisions arrived at intuitively."
>
> Leybourne and Sadler-Smith, 2005

I argued in section one of this book that as the project management profession matures, it is important to move beyond the overweighted focus on technical skills. Technical skills are important, but are not adequate to drive organizational change. Today, the new project environment calls upon project managers to be leaders. Organizations are looking to the project management function to deliver results. Intuition will help deliver those results.

Intuition offers the ability to see holistically what is going on in the project environment—not just tasks and timelines but also emotions, situations, and hidden realities. As a profession, we must do a better job delivering project results. Intuition, when properly deployed, will help raise project management to a new era characterized by greater project success.

YOUR TICKET TO LEARN

You Are Off to a Great Start

I covered a lot of ground in this book. I explained the need for people skills in the profession of project management and that, without people skills, projects are far more likely to fail. I cited just a few of the many research studies proving that people skills correlate to project success more directly than technical skills. As a result, I call on each of us in the profession to step up our attention to the human side of change.

I shared the six disciplines of A Sixth Sense for Project Management® as the tools we can deploy to manage the human side of change. If you read the entire book, you are now familiar with each of the six disciplines: Awareness, Whole Body Decisions™, Clear Communication, Adaptability, Diplomacy and Persistence. Also, you are now familiar with ways these disciplines can be successfully applied in the project environment. This is a fantastic start.

However, it is only a start. The path toward A Sixth Sense for Project Management® is an ongoing journey. When I was in college, I earned my pilot's license. I was very happy the day I received it. I remember sitting in a train on the way back to my home in Chicago feeling proud of the accomplishment. However, I also remember the words of my flight instructor: "Your pilots' license is a ticket to learn." In other words, the license is the beginning of the journey and not the end.

And so it is with managing the human side of change. The six disciplines are skills that must be nurtured and developed. I encourage you to use this book to propel yourself up to the next level. Use it as a reference. Think about the disciplines when you are leading teams. Consider reading more on the topic, talking to colleagues about it, attending our training or webinars, and doing whatever you can to deepen your understanding of the human experience during times of change.

I have done my best to define A Sixth Sense for Project Management® as a set of disciplines. I think it's a very important start. However, there is still something about it that has eluded these disciplines: a higher-level understanding that many experienced people in any profession talk about. I attempted to address this in the chapter on intuition. It's about the airline pilot just knowing which action to take despite what the training guides might say. It's about the surgeon intuitively using an approach that is not in any textbook. It's about the mother fox instinctively shielding her pup moments before a branch falls. This intuition happens in projects too. An example is when the project manager correctly changes course even when the work plan indicates everything is going well.

Projects are about change. Change is about people. People are not simple and are not fully explainable by formulas, charts, graphs, or anything else our rational brain can develop. There is some other deeply profound element of the human experience that is present in projects. Perhaps we see it more directly than people in other professions. We know that we are rewiring people's professional routines. For many people, work is one of their strongest emotional and personal connections.

New scientific equipment, such as Functional Magnetic Resonance Imaging (fMRI), has put us at an exciting moment in human history. fMRI shows changes in blood flow in our brains. This may uncover many mysteries. At Roeder Consulting, we are working hard to keep abreast of the latest developments in order to share it with you. I welcome you to connect with us on the social media sites and come along the journey with us. We will all learn more if we learn together.

There is still so much we do not understand. We know that each of the disciplines plays an important role in working with people. Yet our science still can't explain fully how some of these concepts work. For example, we know some people have an amazing disposition toward spontaneous intuition. That is, they have the ability to perceive things without any seemingly tangible information. We know it happens, but we don't know why. But that does not mean these things are not there. Initially, mankind could not explain why the sun set every night. But it did. Mankind did not know how to start fires. But there were fires. Now mankind can't fully explain the sixth sense. But just like fire and the sun, the sixth sense is waiting for us to figure it out. Join us on the journey.

You Are in the Right Place at the Right Time

In closing, I would like to share with you some research that indicates you are in the right place at the right time. Are you one of those people who says, "I am never in the right place at the right time"? Your luck is about to change.

The World Bank performed research on all of the economic activity around the world. Based on this research, it is estimated that 21 percent of all of the world's economic activity is project-based. It is astounding when you think about it. Twenty-one percent of every financial transaction that occurs is a project. How much of this do you think is professionally managed as a project? I have not seen that statistic, but I suspect it is low. This creates a tremendous opportunity for those of us who manage projects for a living.

Next, consider the following research by the Economist Intelligence Unit. In the research, senior executives were asked the following question: "What capability will be most critical to your company's success in the next five years?" The number-one answer was "ability of key staff to lead and implement change."

Put these two pieces of research together: 21 percent of all the world's economic activity is project-based, and the number-one concern on the mind of organizational chief's is securing people with the ability to manage these projects.

Here's the punch line: if you are able to refine your technical skills, lay on top of it business acumen and the all-important sixth sense people skills, then no one is better equipped than you to fill this gap and help these organizations lead their changes.

In closing, please accept my appreciation for all of the great work you do. If I challenge conventional thinking and constructively criticize the profession, it is in the spirit of raising the bar. I firmly believe we can do better. We must do better. The world needs us to help it change successfully.

ACKNOWLEDGEMENTS

Several years ago, the muscles in my neck began to tighten. I felt my head pulling to the side as the muscles became even tighter over time. Eventually the muscles were in a full-blown contraction that did not stop. I was not able to look straight ahead. Having no idea what was going on, I consulted a doctor. Several specialists later, I was told it was cervical dystonia. As I worked on recovery and the muscles began to loosen, a fascinating phenomenon began to occur. When something happened that caused even the slightest amount of stress or emotional discomfort, I could feel the tugging of my neck muscles. For example, when sitting at the airport and an announcement was made for yet another flight delay, the tug was there. I occasionally felt the tug in project meetings and stakeholder briefings.

Over time, I grew to appreciate this sensation as a sort of high-performance radar that was telling me something important about my environment. This solidified my path toward A Sixth Sense for Project Management®. *Surely, there are things we can all do,* I thought, *to become more sensitive to these signals. Maybe we can learn how to mitigate them. When uncomfortable situations arise, perhaps we can better manage them.* I am grateful that cervical dystonia, in its own way, brought me to this new level of awareness.

Now for the true acknowledgments. My best friend and beautiful wife of 16 years, Elizabeth, masterfully kept everything else on track while I focused my attention on writing, researching, and collecting the various experiences shared on these pages.

My sons Garrett and Parker are a profound source of joy in my life. They continue to teach me every day as I vicariously see the world through their thoughtful perspectives.

Christina Reid, my assistant at Roeder Consulting, became expert at unearthing difficult-to-find books and various facts that appear in the book. Christina also did a magnificent job keeping everything going in the office during the days I removed myself from the scene to focus on writing.

Andrea Turner, a personal friend and a tremendous editor, provided invaluable feedback for this manuscript. How else would I know that commas are supposed to go in so many different places?

I would like to thank several other colleagues at Roeder Consulting who served as sounding boards for many of the key concepts in this book: Dale Christenson, DPM, PMP; Steven Hayward, PhD; Keith Jenkins, MBA, PMP; Steve Martin, MBA, PMP; and Christine Zust, MA.

Many thanks to Dr. Louis Csoka for reviewing select sections for accuracy. Thanks to Dr. Doug Einstein for finding time in his busy schedule to review the brain exhibit in chapter eight.

Julie Dornback patiently and expertly captured the author photograph on the cover. Cindy Kepler worked her artistic magic on the images for the six disciplines and many of the other graphics.

Finally, thanks to everyone who has attended one of Roeder Consulting's programs or who has used our consulting services. I have learned from each of you and continue to do so. Thanks for everything you do.

NOTES

Chapter One: A Profession in Trouble

Roeder Consulting's 90 percent success rate measures our project-based consulting work. We consider a project successful only if the project goal is achieved. For example, in two projects with the same client a new CEO was appointed midstream. He cancelled our projects. This was out of our control. However, we do not count these as successful projects because the project goal was not achieved.

For more information on industry-wide IT project failure rates, see The Standish Group's CHAOS report 2010. This report shows that 32 percent of IT projects succeed by delivering on time, in budget, and within the desired scope. Another 44 percent are "troubled" and 24 percent fail.

To understand the statistical relationship between a variety of project factors, including people skills training and project success rates, see J. Thomas and M. Mullaly, 2008, *Researching the Value of Project Management*, Newtown Square, PA, Project Management Institute.

For more on critical success factors for project success see Dale Christenson, 2007, *The Role of Vision as a Critical Success Element in Project Management*, RMIT University, Melbourne, Australia.

Definition of project management is from the Project Management Institute 2008, *A Guide to the Project Management Body of Knowledge (PMBOK® Guide)*, fourth edition, Newtown Square, PA, Project Management Institute. See section 1.2, page five.

For more information about Barry Z. Posner's research, see "What It Takes to Be a Good Project Manager," *Project Management Journal,* vol. 18, no. 1, 1987, Project Management Institute.

For additional evidence that people skills trump technical skills, see Thomas Lechler, "Empirical Evidence of People as Determinants of Project Success," reprinted in *Projects as Business Constituents and Guiding Motives,* 2000, Kluwer Academic Publishers.

For additional discussion on the importance of people skills, see Bin Jiang's "Key Elements of a Successful Project Manager," *Project Management Journal,* vol. 8, no. 1, 2002, Project Management Institute.

To learn more about variances in people skills requirements by project phase, see Skulmoski and Hartman's "Information Systems Project Manager Soft Competencies: A Project-Phase Investigation," *Project Management Journal,* vol. 41, no. 1, 2009, pp. 61-80, Project Management Institute.

For more information on how professionals from a variety of fields develop and maintain their professional competence, see Graham Cheetham and Geoff Chivers' "The Reflective (and Competent) Practitioner: A Model of Professional Competence Which Seeks to Harmonise the Reflective Practitioner and Competence-based Approaches," *Journal of European Industrial Training,* 22/7, 1998, pp. 267-276. A broad study looking at various professional disciplines, the researchers argue the four areas of competence are knowledge/cognitive, functional, personal/behavioral and values/ethical.

Chapter Two: Birth of A Sixth Sense for Project Management®

Survey results are from a survey conducted in partnership with Northeast Ohio Project Management Institute Chapter. There were 150 respondents to the survey.

For more information on the Project Management Professional (PMP) credential or the Project Management Institute (PMI), see PMI.org.

Chapter Three: A Call to Action for a More Balanced Approach

For more details on how the PMBOK® Guide describes project management and projects, see sections 1.2 and 1.3 of the PMBOK® Guide version 4.0.

For more discussion on Agile project management, see agilemanifesto.org; agilealliance.org; scrumalliance.org; or pmi.org/agile.

To see a discussion on the increased project failure rates, see The Standish Group's CHAOS report 2010.

"PMI", "PMP", "PMBOK", and "PgMP" are registered marks of the Project Management Institute, Inc.

Chapter Four: Awareness

Leonardo da Vinci quote is from *How to Think Like Leonardo da Vinci: Seven Steps to Genius Every Day,* by Michael J. Gelb, page seventy-four, Delta, 1998.

For more information on the concept "thoughts are things," see *Change Your Brain Change Your Life* by Dr. Daniel G. Amen, Three Rivers Press, 1998. In particular, see chapter 5 titled "Enhancing Positive Thought Patterns and Strengthening Connections."

For a plan to visualize success, see *Think and Grow Rich* by Napoleon Hill. Originally published in 1937, this timeless classic discusses specific steps to visualize and achieve successful outcomes.

Chapter Five: Whole Body Decisions™

For more information on the intelligence of the heart, see Doc Childre and Howard Martin's *The HeartMath Solution,* 1999, HarperOne.

For more information on the intelligence of the gut, see Dr. Michael D. Gershom's *The Second Brain,* 1998, Harper.

Interesting brain information can be found in *Your Brain: A User's Guide* by *Time* magazine, 2009, edited by Jeffrey Kluger.

Chapter Six: Communication

For more detail on the challenges of e-mail, see Shawn Adderly's "UI Study: Technology Not Always Best Tool for Communication," *Daily Illini,* August 2, 2010. This article discusses the original research conducted by Gregory Northcraft and Kevin Rockmann.

The Basic Communication Model in Exhibit 6-1 is from *A Guide to the Project Management Body of Knowledge (PMBOK® Guide) - Fourth Edition,* Project Management Institute, Inc., 2008. Copyright and all rights reserved. Material from this publication has been adapted and reproduced with the permission of PMI.

Chapter Seven: Adaptability

J. Thomas and M. Mullaly, 2008, *Researching the Value of Project Management,* Newtown Square, PA, Project Management Institute.

Chapter Eight: Diplomacy

To read more about creating a fair change process, see Joel Brocker's "Why It's So Hard to Be Fair," *Harvard Business Review,* vol. 84, no. 3, March 2006.

For more information on the impact of perceived fairness in wrongful termination lawsuits, see Jerald Greenberg and Allan Lind's, "The Pursuit of Organizational Justice: From Conceptualization to Implication to Application," reprinted in *Industrial and Organizational Psychology,* 2000, Blackwell Publishers.

To learn more about the relationship between medical malpractice lawsuits and the patient/doctor relationship, see Wendy Levinson's "Physician-Patient Communication: The Relationship with Malpractice Claims Among Primary Care Physicians and Surgeons," *Journal of the American Medical Association,* February 19, 1997, vol. 277, no. 7.

For more discussion about the chemicals our bodies release from stress and the impacts of stress, see John Carpi's "Stress: It's Worse Than You Think," *Psychology Today,* January 1, 1996.

For a detailed analysis of how our emotions can overtake us, see Daniel Goleman's *Emotional Intelligence: Why It Can Matter More Than IQ,* Bantam Dell, 1994.

Further research on the amygdala, emotions, and the brain can be found on the website of Joseph LeDoux: cns.nyu.edu/home/ledoux/.

Fascinating research demonstrating the relationship between emotions and activation of the amygdala can be found in Matthew D. Lieberman's "Social Cognitive Neuroscience: A Review of Core Processes," *Annual Review of Psychology,* 2007, 58:259–89.

For more discussion on the ways life events and stress can change our brains and also the role of the amygdala, see chapter two in the report found on the US surgeon general's website: surgeongeneral.gov/library/mentalhealth/chapter2/sec1.html.

Chapter Nine: Persistence

For more discussion about working memory and basil ganglia, see by David Rock and Jeffrey Schwartz's "The Neuroscience of Leadership," *Strategy & Business Magazine,* summer 2006, (pub. by) Booz Allen Hamilton.

To learn more about the effect of observation on people's performance, review Harvard Business School's explanation of the research it conducted at the Hawthorne Works from 1924 to 1933. Elton Mayo led the research. Llibrary.hbs.edu/hc/hawthorne/09.html#nine.

For research discussing how facts may not change opinions, see Brendan Nyhan and Jason Reifler's paper "When Corrections Fail: The Persistence of Political Misperceptions," Springer Science+Business Media, LLC, published online March 30, 2010.

For more discussion on Agile project management, see agilemanifesto.org; agilealliance.org; scrumalliance.org or pmi.org/agile.

Chapter Ten: Intuition

Project Management Institute, 2008, *A Guide to the Project Management Body of Knowledge (PMBOK® Guide)*, fourth edition, Newtown Square, PA, Project Management Institute.

For more on the correlation between people skills and project success see J. Thomas and M. Mullaly, 2008, *Researching the Value of Project Management*, Newtown Square, PA, PMI. Additional studies are cited in chapter one.

The definition of business acumen is from *Wikipedia,* <u>en.wikipedia.org/wiki/ Business acumen</u>.

For more details on how project managers deploy intuition, see S. Leybourn and E. Sadler-Smith, 2005, *The Role of Intuition and Improvisation in Project Management*, International Journal of Project Management.

The definition for intuition is from *Wikipedia,* en.wikipedia.org/ wiki/Intuition_(knowledge).

For Katy Couric's interview of Captain Sullenberger, see –"I Was Sure I Could Do It," youtube.com/watch?v=rZ5HnyEQg7M.

Details of Juan Fangio's intuitive moment are found in "Criminal Investigative Failures: Avoiding the Pitfalls," *The FBI Law Enforcement Bulletin,* findarticles. com/p/articles/mi_m2194/is_9_75/ai_n27100172/

For more details on the unconscious mind see *Wikipedia*, en.wikipedia.org/wiki/ Unconscious_mind.

Chapter Eleven

To see more detail on how it was determined that 21 percent of the world's economic activity is project-based, see Christophe Bredillet's "From the Editor," *Project Management Journal*, vol. 8, no. 2, 2007, page four.

For more detail on the most critical employee skills, see "Talent Wars: The Struggle for Tomorrow's Workforce," a report from The Economist Intelligence Unit, May 2008.

INDEX

U

V

W